22059

D0957127

Living in the Spirit

Library
Oakland S.U.M.

22053

Library
Oakland S.U.M.

Living in the Spirit

by
John MacArthur, Jr.

This book is a gift from the
RICHARD GRAY FAMILY to
Bethany College

MOODY PRESS
CHICAGO

© 1981, 1983 by
JOHN F. MACARTHUR, JR.

Moody Press Edition, 1987

All rights reserved. No part of this book may be reproduced in any form
without permission in writing from the publisher, except in the case of
brief quotations embodied in critical articles or reviews.

All Scripture quotations, unless noted otherwise, are from the *New Scofield
Reference Bible*, King James Version. Copyright © 1967 by Oxford University Press, Inc. Reprinted by permission.

Moody Press, a ministry of the Moody Bible Institute, is designed for edu-
cation, evangelization, and edification. If we may assist you in knowing
more about Christ and the Christian life, please write us without obliga-
tion: Moody Press, c/o MLM, Chicago, Illinois 60610.

Library of Congress Cataloging in Publication Data

MacArthur, John F.
  Living in the Spirit.

  (John MacArthur's Bible studies)
  Includes indexes.
  1. Bible. N.T. Ephesians V, 18-21—Criticism,
interpretation, etc. 2. Spiritual life—Biblical
teaching. I. Title. II. Series: MacArthur, John F.
Bible studies.
BS2695.2.M33   1987   227'.507   87-7741
ISBN 0-8024-5315-5

1 2 3 4 5 6 7 Printing/LC/Year 91 90 89 88 87

Printed in the United States of America

Contents

These Bible studies are taken from messages delivered by Pastor-Teacher John MacArthur, Jr., at Grace Community Church in Panorama City, California. The recorded messages themselves may be purchased as a series or individually. Please request the current price list by writing to:

WORD OF GRACE COMMUNICATIONS
P.O. Box 4000
Panorama City, CA 91412

Or call the following number:
818-982-7000

1
Be Not Drunk with Wine—Part 1

Outline

Introduction
A. The Engine
B. The Ignition Switch
C. The Road Map
D. The Roadblocks
E. The Fuel
   1. The energy
   2. The effect

Lesson
I. The Contrast (v. 18*a*)
  A. The Controversy
  B. The Comparison
    1. The social issue
     a) The Christian's source of joy
     b) The world's source of joy
      (1) Drunkenness destroys
      (2) Drunkenness disqualifies
      (3) Drunkenness discredits
       (*a*) 1 Peter 4:2-3
       (*b*) 1 Corinthians 5:11
       (*c*) 1 Corinthians 6:9-10
    2. The religious issue
     a) The Greek counterfeit
     b) The Roman counterfeit
     c) The Corinthian counterfeit
  C. The Context

Conclusion

Introduction

Ephesians 5:18-20 describes the Spirit-filled life, one of the most important aspects of the Christian walk. Without the constant control of the Spirit of God, the believer cannot live by God's standard. One way to see the book of Ephesians is to view the believer as if he were a high-performance automobile.

A. The Engine

Ephesians 1:1–3:13 describes the believer's inheritance and position in Christ. It is somewhat analogous to the automobile's major source of power—the engine. The believer has been given full power because of his relationship to Christ (Eph. 1:19-21).

B. The Ignition Switch

In Ephesians 3:14-21 Paul describes what can be likened to an ignition switch in a automobile. It does no good to have a high-powered engine if it can't be turned on. As you are controlled by God's Spirit, only then do you begin to understand what it means to live the Christian life. As we mature, God will do "exceedingly abundantly above all that we ask or think, according to the power that worketh in us" (3:20). The power of God in our lives allows us to live a life that is pleasing to Him.

C. The Road Map

Ephesians 4:1–6:9 describes the spiritual route we're to drive. The believer is commanded to move along the path that is worthy of His calling (4:1). The road to Spirit-controlled living differs from the way of the world and involves humility versus pride, unity versus discord, love versus hate, light versus darkness, and wisdom versus foolishness.

D. The Roadblocks

As the believer drives his automobile, he comes across many potential roadblocks (6:10-24). If the Christian lives a worthy life, he will inevitably encounter the schemes of Satan (6:11). The battle is "not against flesh and blood, but against principalities, against powers, against the rulers of the darkness of this world, against spiritual wickedness in high places" (6:12). The only way to defeat the devil is to put on the full armor of God and continually pray (vv. 12-18).

E. The Fuel

1. The energy

The only missing element from the illustration of the automobile is the fuel, the Holy Spirit. Paul said, "Be not drunk with wine, in which is excess, but be filled with the Spirit" (5:18). It would do no good to have an automobile if you didn't have fuel. I once saw a magazine illustration of a farmer who won a car. Since he didn't know what an automobile was supposed to do, when it was delivered to him he hooked his horse to the bumper and rode away in style! There are many Christians who do the same thing. They have a vehicle created by God, intended to be empowered by the fuel of the Holy Spirit, but they end up pulling it along their own way. In Ephesians 5:18 God is saying each believer is to be energized by the Holy Spirit and not by his own efforts.

2. The effect

From Ephesians 5:18–6:9, the apostle Paul describes how the filling of the Holy Spirit affects the believer himself (vv. 19-20), his relationships with others in general (v. 21), and his relationship with his spouse (vv. 22-33), his children (6:1-4), and his coworkers (6:5-9). Living in the Spirit will affect every relationship you have because it is the fuel that allows your spiritual automobile to run properly. It is utter foolishness not to use all the tremendous resources that God has made available to the believer. It is like owning the highest priced vehicle available yet never bothering to put fuel in it. Living the Christian life demands that you be controlled by the Holy Spirit.

Lesson

I. THE CONTRAST (v. 18a)

"And be not drunk with wine."

Before we study how to be filled with the Spirit, we must study Paul's contrast, *not* being drunk with wine. Paul's contrast between drunkenness and being Spirit-filled seems simple on the surface yet presents profound truths.

A. The Controversy

Drinking alcohol is a big issue in the church today. Some Christians say, "No Christian should drink because it's a sin." Others say, "It's obviously not a sin to drink because Jesus and others in the Bible drank wine." Still others say, "The only time you should stop drinking is when it offends a weaker Christian brother." There are perspectives on drinking from one end of the spectrum to the other.

B. The Comparison

In Ephesians 5:15 Paul says, "See, then, that ye walk circumspectly, not as fools but as wise [men]." He also said, "Be ye not unwise but understanding what the will of the Lord is" (v. 17). In verse 18 he gives the third negative command: "And be not drunk with wine, in which is excess, but be filled with the Spirit." In all three verses he is simply paralleling the same idea. The wisest person is the one who does the will of God. Being filled with the Spirit is using wisdom in determining the will of God, whereas being drunk is being out of God's will and acting foolish.

1. The social issue

The United States has a massive alcohol and drug problem. The National Institute on Alcohol Abuse and Alcoholism (NIAAA) has estimated that there are at least 10 million alcoholics in America and at least 3.3 million teenage alcoholics (19 percent of all American teenagers). And statistics are rising rapidly. However, drinking has always been portrayed as a glamorous pastime. Whenever alcohol is advertised in the media, it is usually associated with people of distinction.

Paul is saying that if you're looking for joy and and comfort, seek it in the Holy Spirit, not at the bottom of a bottle. The Holy Spirit should be your only resource for joy and exhilaration.

a) The Christian's source of joy

    (1) Matthew 5:3-12—When Jesus introduced His great Sermon on the Mount, He began by saying, "Blessed [happy] are they . . ."

    (2) Ecclesiastes 3:4—Solomon said, "[There is] a time to laugh."

    (3) Proverbs 17:22—Solomon also said, "A merry heart doeth good like a medicine."

    (4) John 15:11—Jesus said, "These things have I spoken unto you, that my joy might remain in you, and that your joy might be full."

    (5) 1 John 1:4—The apostle John said, "These things write we unto you, that your joy may be full."

    (6) Philippians 4:4—Paul said, "Rejoice in the Lord always; and again I say, Rejoice."

    (7) Psalms 5:11; 32:11; 35:27—David said several times, "Shout for joy."

    (8) Psalm 16:11—David also said, "In thy presence is fullness of joy."

    (9) Luke 2:10—On the day of Jesus' birth an angel said, "Behold, I bring you good tidings of great joy."

b) The world's source of joy

God wants people to experience joy, but He wants them to find it in the right place. People want to be truly happy, but many times their circumstances make them so miserable that they turn to alcohol. I remember asking a young man with a heavy drug addiction, "Do drugs really answer your questions?" He responded, "No, but at least I no longer have to answer any questions because I can't even remember what they are." That is the kind of escape the world calls joy. They are trying to seek joy and happiness in an artificial way.

Advertisers may suggest that alcohol brings comfort, but in Ephesians 5:18 the apostle Paul says the only real Comforter is the Holy Spirit. First Peter 5:7 says to cast "all your care upon him, for he careth for you." Intoxication is never the remedy for the cares of this life. All it does is add more problems to an already guilt-ridden soul.

The world tries to convince us that alcoholism is merely a disease, but it's more than that—it is sin. It is simply the manifestation of human depravity. As any other sin, it needs to be dealt with and confessed. Every mention of drunkenness in the Bible shows a disastrous consequence.

(1) Drunkenness destroys

   (a) Noah became drunk and in his nakedness acted shamelessly (Gen. 9:21).

   (b) Lot became drunk, and his daughters committed incest with him (Gen. 19:30-36).

   (c) Nabal became drunk, and at a crucial time God took his life (1 Sam. 25:36-37).

   (d) Elah became drunk and was murdered by Zimri (1 Kings 16:9-10).

   (e) Ben-hadad and all his allied kings became drunk. Only Ben-hadad escaped slaughter (1 Kings 20:16-21).

(f) Belshazzar became drunk and had his kingdom taken from him (Dan. 5).

(g) The Corinthians got drunk at the Lord's Table. Some died as a result (1 Cor. 11:21-34).

In Scripture drunkenness is always associated with immorality, unrestrained living, and reckless behavior.

(2) Drunkenness disqualifies

Drunkenness disqualifies a man from any form of leadership in the church. An elder or deacon must not be "given to wine" (1 Tim. 3:3, 8; Titus 1:7).

(3) Drunkenness discredits

(a) 1 Peter 4:2-3—Peter said we should no longer live "in the flesh to the lusts of men but to the will of God. For the time past of our life may suffice us to have wrought the will of the Gentiles, when we walked in lasciviousness, lusts, excess of wine, revelings, carousings, and abominable idolatries."

(b) 1 Corinthians 5:11—Paul said, "I have written unto you not to keep company, if any man that is called a brother be a fornicator, or covetous, or an idolater, or a railer, or a drunkard, or an extortioner; with such an one, no, not to eat." Paul was saying that if a person claims to be a believer and yet is a drunkard, you should not even associate with him. What you need to do is share the gospel message with him.

(c) 1 Corinthians 6:9-10—Paul said, "Know ye not that the unrighteous shall not inherit the kingdom of God? Be not deceived: neither fornicators, nor idolaters, nor adulterers, nor effeminate, nor abusers of themselves with mankind, nor thieves, nor covetous, nor drunkards, nor revilers, nor extortioners, shall inherit the kingdom of God."

If a person claims to know Christ yet remains a drunkard, he is deceived and will not inherit the kingdom of God. Paul is not saying that if you get drunk you will automatically lose your salvation. He is saying that a person whose life is characterized by habitual drunkenness is not a true believer. A true believer is characterized by righteousness—not drunkenness. Only God knows who really belongs to Him, and according to His Word, drunkards are not in His kingdom.

If you have a drinking problem, you should examine yourself to see if you are really in the faith (2 Cor. 13:5). Know that God can deliver you from your sinful life. Through the filling of the Holy Spirit, you will find the joy and comfort you seek. If your conversion to Christ is genuine, God will change your life. You will be forgiven of your sins and given a new start. The Lord said, "Though your sins be as scarlet, they shall be as white as snow; though they be red like crimson, they shall be as wool" (Isa. 1:18).

2. The religious issue

The thrust of Paul's teaching on the filling of the Holy Spirit is religious: he is contrasting paganism with Christianity. Pagans believed that one needed to get drunk to reach the highest level of communion with the gods. This is part of what are called the "mystery religions," offshoots of the Greek and Roman mythological religious systems. It is not unlike what occurs today. From men like Timothy Leary to Eastern mystics and occult leaders, people are saying that if you get high on drugs and alcohol, you will reach a greater level of consciousness. Many claim that this is new truth, but it is actually derived from ancient pagan religions. During the apostle Paul's ministry, the Ephesian culture was inundated with many pagan religions.

14

a) The Greek counterfeit

Zeus was considered a great god in Greek mythology. It is said that Zeus assumed human form, impregnated a mortal woman named Semele, and produced a son, Dionysius. Semele decided she had the right to see Zeus in his full glory and entered into his divine presence. She was instantly incinerated. Zeus then snatched the unborn baby from her womb and sewed it into his thigh. He carried the baby until full term and then gave birth. Zeus destined the infant god to become ruler of earth.

According to Greek mythology, there were already sub-gods called Titans who ran the earth, and when they heard of the new ruler, Dionysius, they were infuriated. They stole the baby and ate him. Zeus however, rescued the baby's heart, swallowed it, and gave birth to Dionysius once again. Zeus struck the Titans with lightning, and they were reduced to ashes. Out of those ashes came the human race. Around Dionysius became centered a religion of ascendancy, where human beings attempted to reach a level of divine consciousness. It was filled with ecstasy, wild music, dancing, and sexual perversion—all induced by drunkenness. With a great converging of voices the people would call out to Dionysius, "Come thou Savior." Dionysius became known as the god of wine.

So when Paul said, "Be not drunk with wine," he was not dealing merely with a social problem but a theological one as well. He was dealing directly with Satan's counterfeit religion. Satan captures minds and bodies through the medium of drunkenness.

b) The Roman counterfeit

The Roman name for Dionysius is Bacchus. He is frequently pictured with nymphs and satyrs. The famous bacchanalian feasts were nothing more than drunken orgies. Among the massive ruins of the ancient Near Eastern city of Baalbek is a temple to Bacchus, the god of wine. It is covered with grapes and vines because that was the thrust of their worship.

Paul was saying to the Ephesian church, "Your background was communing with the gods in a state of drunkenness, but if you want to communicate with the true God, you need to be filled with His Spirit. If you want to be raised to the highest level of consciousness, simply enter the presence of God through the filling of the Holy Spirit."

c) The Corinthian counterfeit

The same problem existed in the Corinthian church. They were never able to cut themselves off from the pagan religious systems and divorce themselves from the world. They were cliquish, litigious, proud, egotistical, and uncaring; they pursued vain philosophies and practiced hero worship.

The Corinthian Christians had problems with meat being offered to idols. They also had problems with the gifts of the Spirit, because the pagan religions had corrupted their meaning. That is why it is impossible to properly interpret 1 Corinthians 12-14 without understanding the pagan world of New Testament times. Christianity was being counterfeited in the Corinthian church because they were carrying their former pagan practices into the church. They even corrupted one of the most sacred ordinances that God has given the church—Communion.

The Corinthians were so used to communing with the gods through drunkenness that they came to the Lord's Table drunk. Paul told them they couldn't drink the Communion cup, which is the cup of the Lord, and the cup of drunkenness, which is the cup of demons (1 Cor. 10:21). Their Communion services were characterized by gluttony and drunkenness (1 Cor. 11:19-22). They were conducting their worship the way they used to.

Paul was contrasting the satanic counterfeit of worship with true worship. He didn't want anything to come in the way of what the Spirit wanted to do in the lives of the Ephesians.

C. The Context

I believe Paul is dealing with drunkenness as a religious issue because of the context of Ephesians 5:18-21. He contrasts the pagan liturgy of singing, dancing, and wild parties with true Christian liturgy, which involves speaking with "psalms and hymns and spiritual songs, singing and making melody in your heart to the Lord, giving thanks always for all things unto God and the Father in the name of our Lord Jesus Christ, submitting yourselves one to another in the fear of God" (vv. 19-21).

When Paul said, "Be not drunk with wine, in which is excess, but be filled with the Spirit," he was making a simple contrast. The Greek word for "excess" is *asōtia*, which refers to uncontrolled dissipation or debauchery. Being controlled by alcohol is opposite to being controlled by the Spirit of God.

Conclusion

You are not a person of distinction when you get drunk. I have seen the evils of drunkenness. In the jungles of Ecuador I have watched drunken Indians stagger from one side of the road to the other. I've seen drunkenness in the Arab world and in almost every city I've ever been in. Drunkenness is a part of the curse.

What is controlling your life? Where do you find your joy, exhilaration, and comfort? Do you find it in a bottle? Alcohol is an artificial way of finding those things. If you truly desire to be happy, allow yourself to be controlled and empowered by the Spirit of God. He is the only true source of everlasting joy and comfort.

Focusing on the Facts

1. Without the constant _____ of the Spirit of God, the believer cannot live by God's standard (see p. 8).

2. Describe the illustration used of the book of Ephesians and the different aspects that constitute the illustration (see pp. 8-9).
3. What is one roadblock to living the Spirit-controlled Christian life (see pp. 8-9)?
4. What is the effect of living the Spirit-filled life (see p. 9)?
5. True or false: Drinking alcoholic beverages is a big issue in the church today (see p. 10).
6. How did Paul reason that being drunk with wine is the antithesis of true wisdom (Eph. 5:15, 17; see p. 10)?
7. How is drinking portrayed in the media, and how is it affecting today's society (see p. 11)?
8. The Holy Spirit should be your only resource for _____ and _____. Support your answer with Scripture (see p. 11).
9. True or false: Alcoholism is only a disease (see p. 12).
10. How does the Bible portray drunkenness? Give scriptural references to support your answer (see pp. 12-13).
11. What was the main thrust of Paul's teaching on the filling of the Holy Spirit (see p. 14)?
12. Give the historical background of Paul's command for the Ephesians to be filled with the Spirit (see pp. 14-16).
13. What problems existed in the Corinthian church that were linked to their former pagan practices (see p. 16)?
14. What does true Christian liturgy involve (see p. 17)?
15. What is the opposite of being controlled by alcohol (see p. 17)?

Pondering the Principles

1. Are you controlled by alcohol? Do you desire liquor or drugs more than reading the Word of God, fellowship, or witnessing? If so, examine yourself to see if you are really a Christian. Study the following passages, and if they characterize your life, confess your sin to God, and ask Him to give you new life in Christ: 1 Corinthians 6:9-11, Galatians 5:19-21, and Revelation 21:8.

2. One way to determine if a person is living in the Spirit is to evaluate how much time he spends reading and studying the Word of God. How much time do you spend in the Word? Is it on a daily basis or seldom—if ever? In Scripture, being filled with the Spirit of God and being filled with the Word of God are synonymous. Study the following parallels between the

Spirit of God and the Word of God and determine if your life is controlled by God's Spirit:

Spirit of God	Word of God
Ephesians 5:18	Colossians 1:9-12
John 3:5-7	1 Peter 1:22-25
Titus 3:5-6	Ephesians 5:25-27
1 Corinthians 3:16	Colossians 3:16
1 Peter 1:2	John 17:17
Romans 8:2	John 8:31-36
2 Corinthians 3:5-6	2 Timothy 3:14-17
1 John 4:4	1 John 2:14
Romans 15:13	Romans 15:4
Romans 8:27	Hebrews 4:12

2
Be Not Drunk with Wine—Part 2

Outline

Introduction
A. The Topic
B. The Trouble
  1. The condemnation of drunkenness
    a) Drunkenness disallowed
      (1) Romans 13:13
      (2) Galatians 5:19-21
      (3) 1 Corinthians 6:9-10
      (4) 1 Peter 4:3
      (5) 1 Thessalonians 5:6-7
    b) Drunkenness defined
    c) Drunkenness described
      (1) Proverbs 20:1
      (2) Proverbs 23:20-21, 29-35
      (3) Isaiah 5:11
    d) Drunkenness denounced
      (1) Isaiah 28:7-8
      (2) Isaiah 56:11-12
      (3) Hosea 4:11
  2. The commendation of drinking

The Christian's Wine List
Question 1: Is Drinking Wine Today the Same as in Bible
    Times?
A. The Biblical Words for Wine
  1. *Oinos/yayin*
  2. *Gleukos/tirosh*
  3. *Sikera/shākar*

Introduction

A. The Topic

Ephesians 5:18a describes the topic of drinking and drunkenness. It raises the crucial question of whether a Christian should drink alcohol. Even though it gives a direct command against drunkenness, it does not say that Christians should totally abstain from drinking alcohol.

Not surprisingly, American society has a severe drinking problem. It is proud, self-indulgent, and pleasure-mad, hence filled with guilt, anxiety, and depression. People try both to live it up and forget it all by drinking. Strangely, however, many Christians—who by definition are supposed to be meek, selfless, and filled with the joy of the Lord—seek their comfort from a bottle.

B. The Trouble

A survey showed that 81 percent of all Roman Catholics and 64 percent of all Protestants drink alcohol. The subject of drinking is an important issue in the church. There is much discussion and confusion over the issue. Some people say a Christian should not drink at all because it is sin and absolutely forbidden in Scripture. Others say a Christian can drink in moderation, especially since the Bible indicates believers drank wine. Some Christians go to dinner and wouldn't think of ordering wine, whereas others order wine first and think about dinner later.

I've met certain missionaries who have instructed me to stay in a particular place because the wine is better. I've also met other missionaries who have never consumed alcohol. There is much concern about whether drinking is an emblem of your spirituality; but spirituality isn't a matter of what you drink—it's who you are! What you do in your life is simply a manifestation of who you really are inside.

1. The condemnation of drunkenness

Drunkenness is forbidden in Scripture. It is a sin.

a) Drunkenness disallowed

(1) Romans 13:13—"Let us walk honestly, as in the day; not in reveling and drunkenness."

(2) Galatians 5:19-21—"The works of the flesh are manifest, which are these: adultery, fornication, uncleanness, lasciviousness, idolatry, sorcery, hatred, strife, jealousy, wrath, factions, seditions, heresies, envyings, murders, drunkenness, revelings, and the like; of which I tell you before, as I have also told you in time past, that they who do such things shall not inherit the kingdom of God."

(3) 1 Corinthians 6:9-10—"Know ye not that the unrighteous shall not inherit the kingdom of God? Be not deceived: neither fornicators, nor idolators, nor adulterers, nor effeminate, nor abusers of themselves with mankind, nor thieves, nor covetous, nor drunkards, nor revilers, nor extortioners, shall inherit the kingdom of God."

(4) 1 Peter 4:3—"The time past of our life may suffice us . . . when we walked in lasciviousness, lusts, excess of wine, revelings, carousings." That kind of life-style is part of the darkness of the past.

(5) 1 Thessalonians 5:6-7—"Let us not sleep, as do others, but let us watch and be sober-minded. For they that sleep sleep in the night; and they that are drunk are drunk in the night."

Drunkenness is part of the life-style from which many believers have come. But they have entered into a relationship with Jesus Christ, and drunkenness is not allowed. The Bible sternly warns against drunkenness. A believer is forbidden to be habitually drunk.

b) Drunkenness defined

What does drunkenness mean? It is the point at which alcohol takes over any part of your faculties. There are varying degrees of drunkenness, and I don't profess to know where that fine line is for everyone, but whenever you yield control of your senses to alcohol, you have become drunk.

c) Drunkenness described

(1) Proverbs 20:1—"Wine is a mocker, strong drink is raging, and whosoever is deceived thereby is not wise." A person who becomes drunk is a fool. He may think the wine is doing something good for him, but it is mocking in every way.

(2) Proverbs 23:20-21, 29-35—"Be not among winebibbers, among gluttonous eaters of flesh; for the drunkard and the glutton shall come to poverty, and drowsiness shall clothe a man with rags. . . . Who hath woe? Who hath sorrow? Who hath contentions? Who hath babbling? Who hath wounds without cause? Who hath redness of eyes? They that tarry long at the wine; they that go to seek mixed wine. Look not thou upon the wine when it is red, when it giveth its color in the cup, when it moveth itself aright. At the last it biteth like a serpent, and stingeth like an adder. Thine eyes shall behold strange things, and thine heart shall utter perverse things. Yea, thou shalt be as he that lieth down in the midst of the sea, or as he that lieth upon the top of a mast. They have stricken me, shalt thou say, and I was not sick; they have beaten me, and I felt it not. When shall I awake? I will seek it yet again."

A person who becomes an alcoholic winds up in utter ruin. I've preached many times in skid-row missions and have seen many men clothed in rags because of their drunkenness. Drinking is such a deceiver. It does not produce a person of distinction, as society portrays, but only rags and emptiness.

The most amazing thing about this description of drunkenness is in verse 35: "I will seek it yet again." After all the trouble of drunkenness, people will turn right around and get drunk again. Old Testament commentator Franz Delitzsch said, "The author passes from the sin of uncleanness [vv. 26-28 warn about the harlot and the adulteress] to that of drunkenness; they are nearly related, for drunkenness excites fleshly lust; and to wallow with delight in the mire of sensuality, a man, created in the image of God, must first brutalize himself by intoxication" (*Biblical Commentary on the Proverbs of Solomon*, vol. 2 [reprint, Grand Rapids: Eerdmans, 1970], p. 120).

(3) Isaiah 5:11—"Woe unto them who rise up early in the morning, that they may follow strong drink; who continue until night, till wine inflames them!" One of the characteristics of an alcoholic is that he starts drinking in the morning and continues to drink all night.

d) Drunkenness denounced

(1) Isaiah 28:7-8—In a strong indictment of Ephraim, Isaiah said, "They also have erred through wine, and through strong drink are out of the way. The priest and the prophet have erred through strong drink; they are swallowed up of wine, they are out of the way through strong drink, they err in vision, they stumble in judgment. For all tables are full of vomit and filthiness, so that there is no place clean."

Priests were forbidden to drink while they ministered (Lev. 10:9) because they represented God on earth and if they became drunk, they could easily misjudge or misrepresent God. These priests had made statements that were not true and had given the people wrong judgments, leading them astray. Verse 8 says they were even vomiting right in the place where they drank.

(2) Isaiah 56:11-12—In indicting the watchmen of Israel, Isaiah said, "They are greedy dogs that can never have enough, and they are shepherds that cannot understand; they all look to their own way, every one for his gain, from his quarter. Come, say they, I will fetch wine, and we will fill ourselves with strong drink, and tomorrow shall be as this day, and much more abundant."

These watchmen were supposed to be caring for the people of Israel, yet they remained drunk. God in turn severely indicted them, as He does anyone in a position of spiritual responsibility who negates it by becoming drunk.

(3) Hosea 4:11—"Harlotry and wine and new wine take away the heart." Many times in Scripture, drinking is linked with prostitution.

God forbids drunkenness. Under no circumstances is a believer to yield control of his faculties to the evils of alcohol. All believers have a spiritual responsibility to represent God in the best way possible. Any act of drunkenness, no matter how minimal, violates God's standard of being controlled by the Spirit of God.

2. The commendation of drinking

Drunkenness is directly forbidden by God, yet wine itself is commended in Scripture.

a) Exodus 29:39-40—Moses commanded the children of Israel to offer one lamb in the morning "and the other lamb thou shalt offer at evening: and with the one lamb a tenth part of flour mixed with the fourth part of an hin of beaten oil; and the fourth part of an hin of wine for a drink offering" (cf. Lev. 23:13). Although this wine offering was not for drinking, it was poured out to God as a libation.

b) 1 Chronicles 9:29—Some "were appointed to oversee the vessels, and all the vessels of the sanctuary, and the fine flour, and the wine, and the oil, and the frankincense, and the spices." It is likely they kept a supply of wine in the Temple for drink offerings.

c) Psalm 104:15—The psalmist said that wine "maketh glad the heart of man" (cf. Judges 9:13).

d) Isaiah 55:1—Isaiah said, "Every one that thirsteth, come to the waters, and he that hath no money; come, buy and eat; yea, come, buy wine and milk without money and without price." Wine here is equated with salvation.

e) John 13:26—Jesus dipped a piece of bread in wine, the two elements of the Lord's Supper (cf. 1 Cor. 11:23-26).

f) 1 Timothy 5:23—Paul told Timothy, "Drink no longer water, but use a little wine for thy stomach's sake and thy frequent infirmities."

g) Luke 10:34—When the Good Samaritan found a beaten man on the side of the road, he "went to him, and bound up his wounds, pouring in oil and wine, and set him on his own beast, and brought him to an inn, and took care of him."

h) Proverbs 31:6-7—King Lemuel said, "Give strong drink unto him that is ready to perish, and wine unto those that are of heavy hearts. Let him drink, and forget his poverty, and remember his misery no more." When someone is sick and about to die, Scripture says give him wine as a sedative to ease his pain.

Drinking is seen in Scripture as a possible destroyer of human life but is also seen as an acceptable and sometimes even commendable act. As many other things, wine has a potential for good and evil. Should a Christian drink alcoholic beverages? Does the Bible say anything to help answer this crucial question? The Bible does not forbid drinking wine, but it does give certain principles to determine how to deal with this issue. The following are eight checkpoints to ask yourself if you, as a Christian, should drink alcoholic beverages.

The Christian's Wine List

QUESTION 1: Is Drinking Wine Today the Same as in Bible Times?

Christians who drink point out that wine was commended in the Bible and assume it is therefore acceptable today. If drinking in biblical times is to be used as the basis for drinking today, the wine today should be the same as the wine used then. This deserves careful analysis.

A. The Biblical Words for Wine

1. *Oinos/yayin*

The most common word in the New Testament for wine is the Greek word *oinos*. It is a general word that simply refers to the fermented juice of the grape. The Old Testament equivalent to the Greek word *oinos* is *yayin*, the root of which means to "bubble up" or "boil up." The 1901 Jewish Encyclopedia (vol. 12, p. 533) states that *yayin*, at least in the rabbinic period, was diluted with water.

2. *Gleukos/tirōsh*

The Greek word *gleukos* (from which we get the English word *glucose*) means "new wine." It is used in Acts 2:13 to refer to the apostles on the Day of Pentecost. It says they were "full of new wine." Although it was comparatively fresh and not yet fully aged, it was potentially intoxicating. The mockers in Acts 2:13 were accusing the apostles of being drunk.

The Old Testament word for new wine is *tirōsh*. Hosea 4:11 says "wine [*yayin*] and new wine [*tirōsh*] take away the heart." Drunkenness is the result of drinking this new wine.

28

3. *Sikera/shākar*

The Old Testament word for strong drink is *shākar*, a term that eventually became restricted to intoxicants other than wine. According to the 1901 Jewish Encyclopedia, it refers to unmixed wine. The New Testament equivalent is the Greek word *sikera*.

B. The Historical Data Regarding Wine

1. Unfermented wine

   Because of refrigeration problems in ancient times, wine was often boiled until the liquid evaporated, leaving behind a thick, unintoxicating paste that stored well. It was somewhat similar to modern grape jelly. The people would spread it on bread like a jam, and some still do today in the Middle East.

   a) Pliny the Elder—This Roman historian in his *Natural Histories* said such wine could last as long as ten years. He wrote of wine that had the consistency of honey.

   b) Horace—This Latin poet wrote in his *Odes* of unintoxicating wine that he recommended quaffing underneath the shade (I:18).

   c) Plutarch—This Greek essayist wrote in his *Moralia* that filtered wine neither inflames the brain nor infects the mind and the passions and is much more pleasant to drink. He liked the kind of wine with no alcoholic content.

   d) Aristotle—This Greek philosopher spoke of wine that was so thick it was necessary to scrape it from the skins it was stored in and to dissolve the scrapings in water.

   e) Virgil—This Latin writer spoke of the necessity of boiling down wine.

   f) Homer—The celebrated bard, in the ninth book of *The Odyssey*, tells of Ulysses, who took with him in his visit to the Cyclops a goatskin of sweet, black wine that needed to be diluted with twenty parts of water before being consumed as a beverage.

g) Columella—This Latin agronomist, a contemporary of the apostles, wrote that it was common in Italy and Greece to boil wine. That would not have been done if they had wanted to preserve the alcoholic content.

h) Archbishop Potter—Archbishop Potter, born in 1674, wrote in his *Grecian Antiquities* that the Spartans used to boil down their wines and then drink them four years later (Edinburgh, 1813, vol. 2, p. 360). He referred to Democritus, a celebrated philosopher, and Palladius, a Greek physician, as making similar statements concerning wine at that time. Those ancient authorities referred to the boiled juice of the grape as wine.

i) Professor Donovan—Donovan in his *Bible Commentary* said, "In order to preserve their wines . . . the Romans concentrated the must or grape juice, of which they were made, by evaporation, either spontaneous in the air or over a fire, so as to render them thick and syrupy" (p. 295).

j) The Talmud—The Talmud, the codification of Jewish law, mentions repeatedly that the Jews were in the habit of using boiled wine (e.g., *Erubin* 29a).

k) W. G. Brown—Brown, who traveled extensively in Africa, Egypt, and Asia from 1792 to 1798 said that the wines of Syria are mostly prepared by boiling immediately after they are pressed from the grape until they are considerably reduced in quantity, when they are then put into bottles and preserved for use.

l) Caspar Neumann—Dr. Neumann, professor of chemistry in Berlin, 1795, said, "It is observable that when sweet juices are boiled down to a thick consistency, they not only do not ferment in that state, but are not easily brought into fermentation when diluted with as much water as they had lost in the evaporation, or even with the very individual water that exhaled from them" (Nott, London edition, p. 81). The wine evidently lost much of its intoxicating properties after being reconstituted.

m) Dr. Alexander Russell—Russell, in his *Natural History of Aleppo* (London: G. G. and J. Robinson, 1794), said that the concentrated wine juice, called "dibbs," was brought to the city in skins and sold in the public markets. He said it had the appearance of a coarse honey.

The wine that was consumed in biblical times was not what we know as wine today. It was more of a concentrated grape juice with its intoxicating properties basically removed. You cannot defend wine-drinking today on the basis of wine-drinking in Bible times because the two are totally different.

2. Fermented wine

a) The procedure

Wine stored as a liquid, however, would ferment. Professor Robert Stein, in his article "Wine-drinking in New Testament Times" (*Christianity Today*, 20 June 1975, pp. 9-11), tells us that liquid wine was stored in large jugs called *amphorae*. The pure, unmixed wine would be drawn out of these jugs and poured into large bowls called *kraters*, where it was mixed with water. From these *kraters*, it would then be poured into *kylix*, or cups. Wine would never be served directly from the amphora without first being mixed. And according to other historical data on this period, the mixture could be as high as a 20:1 ratio or lower than 1:1.

b) The perception

Drinking unmixed wine was looked upon by Greek culture as barbaric. Stein quotes Mnesitheus of Athens as saying, "The gods have revealed wine to mortals, to be the greatest blessing for those who use it aright, but for those who use it without measure, the reverse. For it gives food to them that take it and strength in mind and body. In medicine it is most beneficial; it can be mixed with liquid and drugs and it brings aid to the wounded. In daily intercourse, to those who mix and drink it moderately, it gives good cheer; but if you overstep the bounds, it brings violence. Mix it half and half, and you get madness; unmixed, bodily collapse."

As a beverage, wine was always thought of as a mixed drink in Greek culture. The ratio of water might have varied but only barbarians drank it unmixed. Stein cites patristic writings that show the early church served mixed wine.

c) The present

Beer has approximately 4 percent alcohol, wine 9 to 11 percent, brandy 15 to 20 percent, and hard liquor 40 to 50 percent (80-100 proof). So, unmixed wine in biblical times measured at approximately 9 to 11 percent. Mixed wine, at a 3:1 ratio, would therefore be between 2.25 to 2.75 percent. By today's standards, a drink has to exceed 3.2 percent to be considered an alcoholic beverage. The wine the ancients mostly consumed was either completely nonalcoholic or subalcoholic by today's standards. To become drunk with wine in those days you would have to drink all day. That is why the Bible commands elders in the church not to be addicted to much wine (1 Tim. 3:3). With such a low alcoholic content, you would have to purpose to become drunk.

So, is drinking wine today the same as in Bible times? No.

QUESTION 2: Is Drinking Wine Necessary?

Because of the lack of fresh water, it was often necessary to drink wine in biblical times. That is sometimes the case today. If you were in a country where wine was all there was and you were thirsty, you would take whatever was available.

A. The Past Necessity

In the New Testament, the Lord produced wine and spoke about drinking wine (John 2:1-11; Matt. 26:26-29). In the Old Testament as in the New, wine was used out of necessity. This was in a day and age when all they had to drink apart from wine was fruit juice, milk, and water. Due to a lack of refrigeration, even wine mixed from the syrup base, if left standing long enough, could ferment. These people had little choice in deciding what to drink.

B. The Present Preference

Today you can go to a supermarket and buy a variety of nonalcoholic beverages. Many parts of the world have an almost unlimited access to running water. Drinking wine is rarely a necessity today. It is a preference, not a necessity. Perhaps you're afraid your host would be offended if you refuse his wine. But if a group of your friends got together at a party and all decided to scratch behind the left ear, would you scratch behind your left ear because you wanted to feel a part of the group? If everyone on your block decided not to use deodorant, would you join in? That is essentially the same kind of reasoning.

If for some reason you were in a situation where wine was all you had available, you would have little choice but to drink it. You would deal with it as a necessity. But in our society, drinking alcohol is simply and only a preference.

Focusing on the Facts

1. Ephesians 5:18 describes the topic of _____ and _____ (see p. 22).
2. True or false: Many Christians, who by definition are supposed to be meek, selfless, and filled with the joy of the Lord, seek their comfort from a liquor bottle (see p. 22).
3. On what should your spirituality be based (see p. 23)?

4. Is drunkenness forbidden in Scripture? Support your answer (see pp. 23-24).
5. What is the definition of drunkenness (see p. 24)?
6. Any act of _____, no matter how minimal, violates God's standard of being controlled by the Spirit of God (see p. 26).
7. True or false: Drunkenness is directly forbidden by God, but drinking wine is commended in Scripture (see p. 26).
8. How is the subject of drinking seen in Scripture (see p. 27)?
9. What criterion must be met if drinking in biblical times is to be sufficient reason for drinking today (see pp. 27-28)?
10. List the different words used for wine in the Bible, and explain each (see pp. 28-29).
11. What is the difference between mixed and unmixed wine (see pp. 28-29)?
12. What was the difference between wine stored as a solid and wine stored as a liquid (see pp. 29-31)?
13. How was drinking unmixed wine looked upon in Greek culture? in the early church (see p. 31)?
14. What was the approximate alcoholic content of wine during biblical times (see p. 32)?
15. Is drinking wine necessary today (see p. 32)?
16. In our society, drinking alcohol is _____ and _____ a preference (see p. 33).

Pondering the Principles

1. The wine spoken of in Bible times is not the same as the wine today. Wine today is not mixed with water and can be intoxicating. The wine people predominately drank during Bible times was mixed with water and was largely unintoxicating. Have you considered those principles in deciding whether to drink? The Bible gives examples of people in positions of spiritual responsibility who abstained from alcohol. Study the following passages, and ask God to make clear to you whether you should abstain from drinking: Leviticus 10:8-11, Judges 13:3-4, and Luke 1:14-15.

2. The Bible condemns drunkenness but also commends the occasional use of wine. However, there is one instance apart from drunkenness when drinking is forbidden: when it causes a fellow believer to stumble (Rom. 14:1-23; 1 Cor. 8:9-13). Are

you using your Christian liberty to drink wine but at the same time causing a brother to stumble? Evaluate your actions with the preceding passages, and determine if you are causing anyone to stumble.

3
Be Not Drunk with Wine—Part 3

Outline

Review
The Christian's Wine List
Question 1: Is Drinking Wine Today the Same as in Bible
    Times?
Question 2: Is Drinking Wine Necessary?

Lesson
Question 3: Is Drinking Wine the Best Choice?
A. The Separation
B. The Standard
    1. The higher standard for Old Testament priests
    2. The higher standard for kings and princes
    3. The higher standard for those taking the Nazirite vow
    4. The higher standard for New Testament church leaders
Question 4: Is Drinking Wine Habit-Forming?
A. The Principle
B. The Possibility
Question 5: Is Drinking Wine Potentially Destructive?
A. The Biblical Evidence
    1. New Testament Scriptures
    2. Old Testament Scriptures
B. The Statistical Evidence
    1. Mental destruction
    2. Physical destruction

Question 6: Is My Drinking Wine Offensive to Other
    Christians?
A. The General Principle
B. The Specific Principle
    1. The offended brother
    2. The weaker brother
    3. The loving brother
Question 7: Will Drinking Wine Harm My Christian
    Testimony?
A. Drinking Among the Saved
B. Drinking Among the Unsaved
Question 8: Am I Absolutely Certain Drinking Wine Is Right?
A. The Conviction
B. The Conscience

Conclusion

Review

THE CHRISTIAN'S WINE LIST

QUESTION 1: Is Drinking Wine Today the Same as in Bible
Times? (see pp. 28-32)

QUESTION 2: Is Drinking Wine Necessary? (see pp. 32-33)

Lesson

QUESTION 3: Is Drinking Wine the Best Choice?

A Christian is constantly faced with choices. The Bible doesn't
speak directly against smoking, but that doesn't make it the
best choice for a believer. A Christian has the option to drink
coffee, but many abstain because of its negative effects on the
body. The same is true for drinking wine. A Christian has the
liberty to drink it, but is that the best choice?

A. The Separation

God called His people Israel to separate themselves from evil. There were higher standards for those with greater leadership responsibilities. With the higher rank came greater consequences and guilt for sin. James 3:1 says, "Be not many teachers, knowing that we shall receive the greater judgment." Likewise, Jesus said, "From everyone who has been given much shall much be required" (Luke 12:48, NASB*). When you sin as a leader in the church, the ramifications of your sin are far-reaching.

B. The Standard

1. The higher standard for Old Testament priests

God established standards for His people, but He called certain men to live above those standards. Leviticus 10:9 gives the standard for priests: "Do not drink wine nor strong drink, thou, nor thy sons with thee, when ye go into the tabernacle of the congregation, lest ye die." Some Bible commentators think this command applied only when the priests ministered inside the Tabernacle. Others believe the command applied to their entire lives. But either way the priests were called to minister for God and abstain from alcohol. God wanted their minds clean, clear, and pure.

2. The higher standard for kings and princes

Proverbs 31:4-5 says, "It is not for kings to drink wine, nor for princes strong drink, lest they drink, and forget the law, and pervert the justice of any of the afflicted." God didn't want their judgment, like the priests, to be clouded. According to verse 6, strong drink was given only to those who were perishing. It was a sedative for their pain. Regular wine was given to those who were heavy of heart. There was to be a greater level of consecration in the leadership of the country.

*New American Standard Bible.

3. The higher standard for those taking the Nazirite vow

   Numbers 6:1-5 says, "The Lord spoke unto Moses, saying, Speak unto the children of Israel, and say unto them, When either man or woman shall separate themselves to vow a vow of a Nazirite, to separate themselves unto the Lord; he shall separate himself from wine and strong drink, and shall drink no vinegar of wine, or vinegar of strong drink, neither shall he drink any liquor of grapes, nor eat moist grapes, or dried. All the days of his separation shall he eat nothing that is made of the vine tree, from the kernels even to the husk. All the days of the vow of his separation there shall no razor come upon his head."

   a) The choice

   Certain people in the congregation of Israel chose to abstain from alcohol. Anyone could choose the higher standard of the Nazirite vow.

   b) The consecration

   The word *Nazirite* comes from the Hebrew word *nazir*, which means "the consecrated one." A Nazirite then was someone who was wholly dedicated to the Lord.

   c) The character

   The person taking the Nazirite vow would no longer cut his hair or drink wine. The highest level of consecration involved total abstinence. Someone who took a Nazirite vow was stepping up to a higher level of commitment and thus identifying with kings, princes, and priests. A Nazirite vow could last for thirty, sixty, ninety days—or even for life.

   There are three people mentioned in the Bible who were Nazirites for life: Samuel (1 Sam. 1:11, 22), Samson (Judg. 13:4-7), and John the Baptist (Luke 1:15). Jesus Himself called John the Baptist the greatest man who ever lived up to his time (Matt. 11:11).

d) The count

Anyone in Israel could take the Nazirite vow. It is unknown exactly how many Nazirites there were in Israel but is likely there were many. God said, "I raised up of your sons for prophets, and of your young men for Nazirites. Is it not even thus, O ye children of Israel?" (Amos 2:11). God was saying He raised up prophets and Nazirites for a higher standard of life among the people.

e) The corruption

Although God raised up men and women to take the Nazirite vow, many in Israel began to corrupt them. Amos goes on to say, "But ye gave the Nazirites wine to drink, and commanded the prophets, saying, Prophesy not" (v. 12). They desecrated the Nazirites and the prophets. The Nazirites were enticed into disobedience by the people. Instead of wanting to attain to the highest level of devotion, the people wanted to drag those who were there to the lowest level in their society.

f) The contrast

Jeremiah contrasts the disobedience of Israel with the obedience of the Rechabite family (cf. Jer. 35:2-6). The Rechabites said, "We will drink no wine; for Jonadab, the son of Rechab, our father, commanded us, saying, Ye shall drink no wine, neither ye, nor your sons forever" (v. 6). The entire family took a vow of total abstinence from wine. They desired the highest level of devotion to God, and when bowls of wine were set before them, they refused to drink. They remained strong in their commitment to the Lord.

4. The higher standard for New Testament church leaders

The New Testament presents little change in God's standard for leadership. Peter said, "Ye [believers] are a chosen generation, a royal priesthood, an holy nation, a people of his own, that ye should show forth the praises of him who hath called you out of darkness into his marvelous light" (1 Pet. 2:9). All Christians have been called to the highest level of service for God and are expected to make the best choices.

a) The leadership in general

> Since the priests, Nazirites, kings, judges, and other rulers of Israel were to be clear-minded at all times, the Lord surely does not have lower standards for leaders in the church, the Body of Christ. Paul told Timothy that a leader in the church must not be "given to wine" (Gk., *paroinon*), which literally means, "being beside wine" (1 Tim. 3:3).

> A leader in the church is not to be tempted or enticed by wine. "Must" in 1 Timothy 3:2 is from the Greek particle *dei* and carries the meaning of logical necessity rather than moral obligation. If a man desires the office of elder, it is only logical that he not be a habitual drinker.

b) Timothy in particular

> In 1 Timothy 5:23 Paul tells Timothy, "Drink no longer water, but use a little wine for thy stomach's sake and thy frequent infirmities." If Timothy normally drank wine, Paul most likely would not have had to tell him that. Paul's recommendation was for medicinal purposes. Timothy had probably also taken himself to a higher level of commitment as a leader in the church of Jesus Christ by abstaining from wine.

The Bible prescribes a high standard for those who aspire to positions of spiritual leadership. Perhaps the best choice is to align yourself with priests, kings, princes, Nazirites, and current church leaders. Every believer is to present his body as a living and holy sacrifice to God in an act of spiritual worship (Rom. 12:1-2). Everyone should then consider making the best and highest choice of abstaining from alcoholic beverages. Maybe the best choice is to stand with those who have made a decision to give their whole lives to Jesus Christ.

QUESTION 4: Is Drinking Wine Habit-Forming?

A. The Principle

Many of the habits we form are beneficial. But some activities may become unprofitable habits. Paul said, "All things are lawful unto me, but all things are not expedient" (1 Cor. 6:12). He in effect is saying, "There are things I could do, but they would trip me up or entangle me." This passage can aptly be applied to the danger of alcohol addiction.

B. The Possibility

Paul also said, "All things are lawful for me, but I will not be brought under the power of any" (1 Cor. 6:12b). Alcohol has the potential of bringing you under its power. It easily produces an overpowering dependency that distracts one's attention and interferes with brain and bodily functions. Not only would a Christian want to avoid sin but also the potential for sin. Food is somewhat similar to wine in its potential for sin. If you cannot control your intake of food, you are in danger of becoming gluttonous. Unlike wine, food is a necessity, but the same principle applies. A good practice is to vary your eating habits and occasionally abstain from food completely to make sure you are in control of what you eat and not vice versa. The Christian is to be controlled by the Spirit, not by ungodly influences that can lead him to sin.

QUESTION 5: Is Drinking Wine Potentially Destructive?

A. The Biblical Evidence

1. New Testament Scriptures

   a) Ephesians 5:18—Paul uses a strong word in Ephesians 5:18 to describe the destructiveness of drunkenness. *Asōtia* can be translated "excess" or "dissipation" and literally means "that which is unable to be saved." It was used of a person who was hopelessly and incurably sick based on loose, profligate living.

b) Luke 15:13—Here *asōtia* is used of the prodigal son, who engaged in "riotous living."

2. Old Testament Scriptures

   a) Proverbs 20:1—Solomon said, "Wine is a mocker, strong drink is raging, and whosoever is deceived thereby is not wise" (cf. Prov. 4:17; 21:17; 23:21, 29-35).

   b) Genesis 9:21—Noah "drank of the wine, and became drunk; and he was uncovered within his tent." Where there is drunkenness there is immorality (cf. Gen. 19:30-35).

   c) Deuteronomy 21:20—Moses instructed parents of rebellious children to say, "This, our son, is stubborn and rebellious. He will not obey our voice; he is a glutton, and a drunkard." Drunkenness is often accompanied by gluttony and rebellion.

   d) Isaiah 28:7-8—Isaiah said, "The priest and the prophet have erred through strong drink; they are swallowed up of wine, they are out of the way through strong drink, they err in vision, they stumble in judgment. For all tables are full of vomit and filthiness, so that there is no place clean." Wine and strong drink corrupted the prophets and the priesthood.

   e) Joel 1:5; 3:3—Joel said, "Awake, ye drunkards, and weep; and wail, all ye drinkers of wine, because of the new wine; for it is cut off from your mouth. . . . They have cast lots for my people, and have given a boy for an harlot, and sold a girl for wine, that they might drink." God withdrew from the Israelites the right to drink. They had sunk to the level of selling a person for wine.

   f) Hosea 7:5—Hosea said, "In the day of our king, the princes have made him [the king] sick with skins of wine." Ephraim's iniquity was linked to wine.

   g) Amos 2:8—Amos said the Israelites laid "themselves down upon clothes laid to pledge by every altar, and they drink the wine of the condemned in the house of their god." They oppressed the poor in their drunken state (4:1). Amos agonized over the debauchery that comes from drunkenness and wine.

    h) Habakkuk 2:15-16—Habakkuk warned, "Woe unto him that giveth his neighbor drink, that puttest thy wineskin to him, and makest him drunk also, that thou mayest look on their nakedness! Thou art filled with shame for glory; drink thou also, and let thy shame come upon thee; the cup of the Lord's right hand shall be turned unto thee, and shameful spewing shall be on thy glory." Habakkuk was saying that if you make your neighbor drunk, God will spew on you His cup of judgment.

The Christian must ask himself if it is wise for him to have any part of something that has such great potential for destruction and sin.

B. The Statistical Evidence

(The information below is documented in Dr. S. I. McMillen's *None of These Diseases* [Old Tappan, N.J.: Revell, 1963], pp. 22-28.)

1. Mental destruction

    It has been estimated that 20 percent of all patients admitted into mental hospitals have a problem with alcohol.

2. Physical destruction

    a) To yourself

        Alcoholism causes cirrhosis (hardening) of the liver, which in turn can cause a ballooning of the veins in the esophagus. The thinned-out veins are then prone to rupture when food is swallowed, potentially causing a serious or even fatal hemorrhage.

b) To others

Alcohol is not only potentially harmful to the people who drink, but it also has a detrimental effect on the lives of innocent people. A study of autopsy findings in Middlesex County, New Jersey, showed alcohol was a factor in 41.2 percent of violent deaths. A study in Delaware indicated that alcohol is the cause of nearly 50 percent of traffic deaths. In New York City a joint study made by the State Department of Health and Cornell University revealed that 73 percent of the drivers responsible for the accidents in which they died had been drinking. In Westchester County, New York, blood tests were done on eighty-three drivers who were killed in single-vehicle accidents. The tests revealed that 79 percent of those drivers were under the influence of alcohol.

QUESTION 6: Is My Drinking Wine Offensive to Other Christians?

Some may well say, "I am free in Christ. I don't want to get into legalistic bondage because someone might not be able to handle drinking alcohol." However, a Christian who is able to drink in moderation is not able to guarantee that his example will not cause a weaker Christian to try drinking and become addicted. Not only that but a former drunk who becomes a Christian will often associate many immoral and corrupt activities with drinking, and to see a fellow Christian drink most likely would offend his conscience.

A. The General Principle

The apostle Paul laid out a general principle in 1 Corinthians 8:9 that can be applied in many different instances. He said, "Take heed, lest by any means this liberty of yours becomes a stumbling block to them that are weak." A believer may very well have the liberty, maturity, and strength to drink in moderation, but he might also set the wrong example for someone who cannot handle any type of drinking. Our freedom in Christ stops when it begins to harm others, especially fellow believers. In Paul's time drunkenness was commonly associated with pagan religions. Those who came to Christ did not want to eat meat

46

offered to idols (the context of 1 Cor. 8) any more than they wanted to be looked upon as drinkers.

B. The Specific Principle

In Romans 14:13-21 Paul gives a more specific principle that applies to the Christian's use of his liberty. Paul said not to let any "man put a stumbling block or an occasion to fall in his brother's way. . . . If thy brother be grieved with thy food [or drink], now walkest thou not in love. Destroy not him with thy food [or drink], for whom Christ died. Let not then your good be evil spoken of" (vv. 13, 15-16).

1. The offended brother

Most of the Gentile Christians would associate drunkenness with debauchery, immorality, gluttony, and all sorts of evil. Jewish believers tended to say, "Drink up! It's no big deal to drink." The Gentile believers were often deeply offended because they believed they didn't have the freedom to drink because of their old life-style. That's what Romans 14:13-21 is trying to avoid. Our freedom in Christ should not be cherished above the welfare of another believer. Paul said believers are to "follow after the things which make for peace, and things with which one may edify another" (v. 19).

2. The weaker brother

There is another category of people—those who simply cannot handle alcohol at all. They might see another Christian drinking, assume drinking must be all right, and become addicted to alcohol. A believer has no control over who might follow his example and end up with a destroyed life.

3. The loving brother

Paul said, "If thy brother be grieved with thy food, now walkest thou not in love. . . . For the kingdom of God is not food and drink, but righteousness, and peace, and joy in the Holy Spirit" (v. 15, 17). Christians are supposed to build up their fellow believers and not tear them down. Paul ends by saying, "For food destroy not the work of God. All things indeed are pure; but it is evil for that man who eateth with offense. It is good neither to eat meat, nor to drink wine, nor anything by which thy brother stumbleth, or is offended, or is made weak" (vv. 20-21). If your drinking offends others, it's better to abstain. You might go through your entire life adjusting to other people, but God can use that to mold you into the person He wants you to be.

QUESTION 7: Will Drinking Wine Harm My Christian Testimony?

A. Drinking Among the Saved

Some people think they can better reach out to drinkers if they themselves drink. However, Paul said, "Let not . . . your good be evil spoken of" (Rom. 14:16). It is possible for you to have a pure motive in drinking, but it may also offend your fellow believers. Drinking might make us more acceptable in some circles, but our lack of concern for fellow Christians would work against any positive witness we might give. If we want to reach people who are not saved, as well as give an encouraging example to those who are, we will not do anything that would cause them to be offended. In my own ministry, I don't want anyone to be disturbed or misled by my actions. I often ask myself, *Will I hurt others with what I am about to do?*

B. Drinking Among the Unsaved

Paul said, "Whether, therefore, ye eat, or drink, or whatever ye do, do all to the glory of God. Give no offense, neither to the Jews, nor to the Greeks, nor to the church of God; even as I please all men in all things, not seeking mine own profit, but the profit of many, that they may be saved" (1 Cor. 10:31-33). We are not to offend believers or the unsaved. If you want to reach the unsaved, let them see a difference in your life. God has established three standards: (1) glorify God, (2) offend no one, and (3) make sure the unsaved sense a difference in your life-style.

QUESTION 8: Am I Absolutely Certain Drinking Wine Is Right?

If you are convicted in any way about your drinking, that may be reason enough to stop.

A. The Conviction

A man once said to me, "I occasionally have a beer with the boys. Is that wrong?" I replied, "What do you think?" He said, "Well, I don't think it's wrong, but it bothers me." "Do you like being bothered?" I asked. "No, I don't," he said. "You know how to stop being bothered, don't you?" I continued, to which he gave the obvious answer, "Yes. Stop drinking."

Paul says in Romans 14:23, "He that doubteth is condemned if he eat, because he eateth not of faith; for whatever is not of faith is sin." Are you absolutely sure it's right to drink? If you have any conviction about your actions, you must deal with it. If you can't do something with a guilt-free conscience, don't do it. Ignoring your doubts will push you into deeper self-condemnation and self-imposed guilt.

B. The Conscience

Conscience is a God-given alarm that guards against sin. Whenever we go against it, we weaken it, making it less reliable. Continually going against your conscience will make it "seared . . . as with a branding iron" (1 Tim. 4:2, NASB). When that happens, you lose a powerful agent God has bestowed to lead the believer (cf. 1 Tim. 1:5, 19).

Conclusion

If you want to be a wise Christian, you must deal with the issue of whether you should drink. Ask yourself the following questions: Is drinking wine the same as in Bible times? Is it necessary? Is it the best choice? Is it habit-forming? Is it potentially destructive? Is it offensive to other Christians? Is it harmful to my testimony? The final question is the most important: Can I do it before others and before God, confident it is right?

Focusing on the Facts

1. A Christian has the _____ to drink (see p. 38).
2. True or false: There were higher standards in the Old Testament for those who had greater leadership responsibilities (see p. 39).
3. What was the standard for the Old Testament priesthood concerning wine and strong drink? Why did God impose that standard (Lev. 10:9; see p. 39)?
4. What was the standard for kings and princes (Prov. 31:4-5; see p. 39)?
5. What was the Nazirite vow, and who could take it (Num. 6:1-5; see pp. 40-41)?
6. The person taking the Nazirite vow would no longer _____ his _____ or _____ any _____ (see p. 40).
7. How long could a Nazirite vow last (see p. 40)?
8. Name the people mentioned in the Bible who were probably Nazirites for life. Support your answer with Scripture (see p. 40).
9. What did the children of Israel do to corrupt many who had taken the Nazirite vow (Amos 2:11-12; see p. 41)?
10. Who were the Rechabite family, and why were they singled out in Scripture (Jer. 32:2-6; see p. 41)?
11. What is the New Testament standard for church leaders concerning the drinking of wine (see pp. 41-42)?
12. If a man desires the office of elder, it is only logical that he not be an _____ drinker (see p. 42).
13. Why did Paul tell Timothy to drink wine (see p. 42)?
14. Is drinking wine habit-forming? Explain your answer (see p. 43).
15. What does Paul mean when he uses the word *excess* in Ephesians 5:18 (see p. 43)?
16. Describe the potential destructiveness of alcohol. Give examples from Scripture to support your answer (see pp. 44-45).
17. Describe the potential mental and physical effects of drinking alcohol (see pp. 45-46).
18. Where does our freedom in Christ end (see p. 46)?

19. What was the general difference in attitude concerning alcohol between Jewish and Gentile believers in Paul's time (see p. 47)?
20. Could drinking wine harm your Christian testimony (see p. 48)?
21. What are three standards God has established to guide a Christian's actions (1 Cor. 10:31-33; see p. 48)?
22. If you are _____ in any way about your drinking, that may be reason enough to _____ (see p. 49).
23. What will occur if you act against your conscience (see p. 49)?

Pondering the Principles

1. The Bible prescribes a high standard for those who aspire to positions of spiritual leadership. The Old Testament priests, kings, princes, and those taking the Nazirite vow all committed themselves to abstaining from drinking any alcoholic beverages. Do you aspire to a position of leadership within the church? The best choice for you might be to align yourself with those who abstain from alcohol. Read slowly through 1 Timothy 3 as you seek God's will in this matter.

2. Page 49 summarizes the eight questions on the Christian's Wine List. Ask yourself those questions again and answer them to the best of your ability. Pray for God to make clear what is right for *you* regarding alcohol.

4
Be Filled with the Spirit—Part 1

Outline

Introduction
A. The Core
B. The Confusion

Review
 I. The Contrast (v. 18*a*)

Lesson
II. The Command (v. 18*b*)
   A. The Misconceptions of Being Filled with the Spirit
      1. The possession of the Holy Spirit
      2. The baptism of the Holy Spirit
      3. The indwelling of the Holy Spirit
         a) Ephesians 4:30
         b) 1 Thessalonians 5:19
         c) Galatians 2:20
         d) John 7:37-39
   B. The Meaning of Being Filled with the Spirit
      1. A continuous action
      2. A comparative analysis
         a) Pressure
         b) Permeation
            (1) The salt principle
            (2) The Fizzie principle
            (3) The control principle
               (*a*) In general
                  i) John 16:6
                  ii) Luke 5:26
                  iii) Luke 6:11

    (b) In specific
       i) Jesus
       ii) Stephen
       iii) Paul
C. The Means of Being Filled with the Spirit
  1. Surrendering your life to Christ
  2. Studying the Word of Christ
  3. Standing in the presence of Christ
    a) Peter before Pentecost
      (1) Miraculous works
      (2) Miraculous words
      (3) Miraculous courage
    b) Peter after Pentecost
      (1) Miraculous words
      (2) Miraculous works
      (3) Miraculous courage

Conclusion

Introduction

A. The Core

Paul says in Ephesians 5:18, "Be not drunk with wine, in which is excess, but be filled with the Spirit." The key to rightly living the Christian life is being controlled by the Holy Spirit, who provides energy for walking "worthy of the vocation to which ye are called" (Eph. 4:1). Unless a believer is controlled by the Spirit of God, he can never walk in humility, love, unity, light, and wisdom. The life of God in the soul of man is the only way by which a person can live a righteous life. To walk without the spirit is to walk without wisdom (cf. Eph. 5:15-17).

B. The Confusion

Many people are confused about what it means to be filled with the Holy Spirit. Some people think you must have some kind of ecstatic experience and speak in tongues, while others approach it stoically. They simply recognize that the Holy Spirit is present but think He makes little or no impact. Both are wrong. The filling or controlling of the

Holy Spirit is a profound reality in the believer's life, and understanding it can change your life.

Review

I. THE CONTRAST (v. 18*a*; see pp. 7-17)

Lesson

II. THE COMMAND (v. 18*b*)

"Be filled with the Spirit."

Within the Greek language is the indicative mood, which is a statement of fact, and the imperative mood, which states a command. Ephesians 5:18 is an emphatic imperative and is literally translated, "Be being kept filled with the Spirit." It is a command that includes the idea of conscious continuation. Being continually filled with the Spirit is not an option for the believer but a biblical mandate. No Christian can fulfill God's will for his life apart from being filled with the Spirit.

A. The Misconceptions of Being Filled with the Spirit

Much material is in print today that states you can be a Christian but don't necessarily have to be obedient to God. Some teach that simply getting into the kingdom is all that really matters. They consider what one might do in obedience to the Lord through the power of the Spirit is merely some sort of spiritual "extra credit."

However, to resist the filling and control of the Holy Spirit is flagrant disobedience, and to deny or minimize its importance is to stand rebelliously against the clear teaching of God's own Word. Every Christian falls short of God's standards and will sometimes fall into sin and indifference, but those who continually exist in such a state are obviously not Christians. The Holy Spirit has given us a new nature.

What About "Carnal" Christians?

Many people divide humanity into three categories: one is called the "natural man," who is unsaved and on his way to hell (1 Cor. 2:14); the next is the "spiritual man," who is a Christian walking in the truth (1 Cor. 2:15-16); and the last is the "carnal man," who says he's a Christian but is not obedient to God (1 Cor. 3:1-4). But that interpretation is out of harmony with the balance of Scripture. God has commanded every true believer to be obedient to His commands and be controlled by His Spirit (e.g., John 14:15-26). Anything less than that is flagrant disobedience.

In Scripture, the words *carnal* and *fleshly* most often refer to unsaved people and not Christians. The carnal mind as referred to in Romans 8:5-8 directly defies God, which is not at all characteristic of a true believer: "They that are after the flesh do mind the things of the flesh; but they that are after the Spirit, the things of the Spirit. For to be carnally minded is death, but to be spiritually minded is life and peace. Because the carnal mind is enmity against God; for it is not subject to the law of God, neither, indeed, can be. So, then, they that are in the flesh cannot please God." The word *carnal* in this passage can be understood only as referring to the unsaved. So a "carnal Christian" is a contradiction in terms.

Paul chided the Corinthians, saying, "I brethren, could not speak unto you as unto spiritual, but as unto carnal, even as unto babes in Christ. I have fed you with milk, and not with solid food; for to this time ye were not able to bear it, neither yet now are ye able" (1 Cor. 3:1-2). For one-and-a-half years, the apostle Paul had taught the Corinthians. Now he was writing them as much as five years later, so they had been believers for approximately six years. The problem of the Corinthian church was not their infancy but their disobedience, which included divisions, envying, and strife. Paul was saying they were acting like unbelievers. Therefore he gave them this warning: "Examine yourselves, whether you are in the faith; prove yourselves. Know ye not yourselves how Jesus Christ is in you, unless you are discredited?" (2 Cor. 13:5).

There may be Christians who fall into sin and act carnally, but carnality is predominately characterized by unbelievers, because they are totally unable to please God (cf. Heb. 11:6). Hebrews 12:14 declares that no man will see the Lord without holiness.

If a person's life is not characterized by righteousness, the entire book of 1 John declares that he is not truly saved. The person with a disobedient nature is not walking in the Spirit and therefore does not possess the Spirit—in which case he is not a Christian (Rom. 8:9). Submission to the will of God, to Christ's lordship, and to the guiding of the Spirit is an essential—not optional—part of true saving faith. True Christians—those with genuine faith—will not be content with being in a "carnal" category. They will not be satisfied with remaining in a state of habitual disobedience. A person who has no desire for obedience has no legitimate claim on salvation. If you are truly saved, the only thing to do with a command such as "Be filled with the Spirit" is to obey it!

1. The possession of the Holy Spirit

   Every Christian possesses the Holy Spirit in all His fullness from the moment he believes. As was mentioned above, there is no such thing as a Christian without the Holy Spirit. Romans 8:9 says, "If anyone does not have the Spirit of Christ, he does not belong to Him" (NASB). I heard a person say, "I have been a Christian for a long time, but I just found out that I didn't really have the Holy Spirit. Since then, I asked God, and He gave me the Holy Spirit, and now my entire life has changed." I understood what he was trying to say—that he now realized what obedience to God was all about—but there is simply no such thing as a Christian without the Holy Spirit. When you become a child of God, He takes up residence by putting His Spirit within you, and as a result you will be obedient to Him. Every Christian possesses the Holy Spirit in all His fullness. A Christian does not receive the Holy Spirit in bits and pieces. You do not even have to ask for more of the Spirit, because He is all there at salvation.

2. The baptism of the Holy Spirit

   Even to the immature, worldly Corinthian believers, Paul said, "For by one Spirit were we all baptized into one body, whether we be Jews or Greeks, whether we be bond or free; and have been all made to drink into one Spirit" (1 Cor. 12:13). All believers have received the Holy Spirit and been baptized into the Body of Christ.

There are seven specific references for the phrase "baptism of the Holy Spirit" (Matt. 3:11; Mark 1:8; Luke 3:16; John 1:33; Acts 1:5; 11:16; 1 Cor. 12:13). The believer is never commanded to be baptized by the Spirit because that occurs at salvation. Although not specifically referring the the phrase "baptism of the Holy Spirit," the following passages speak metaphorically about the same theological reality of being placed (baptized) into the Body of Christ: Romans 6:3-5, Galatians 3:27, and Colossians 2:11-12. Christ—the baptizer—through the agency of the Holy Spirit places you in His Body at the moment of salvation. The baptism of the Holy Spirit is a theological reality. You do not feel it physically, nor do you see or hear it.

3. The indwelling of the Holy Spirit

Paul did not accuse the Corinthians of being immature and sinful because they did not yet have the Holy Spirit. He didn't exhort them to seek the Spirit to remedy the situation. Rather he reminded them that each one of them already possessed the Holy Spirit: "What? Know ye not that your body is the temple of the Holy Spirit who is in you?" (1 Cor. 6:19). Even when a Christian falls into sin, the Holy Spirit is there convicting him, and it is that very fact that makes his sin even worse. The Corinthians were not sinning because of the Holy Spirit's absence but in spite of His presence.

a) Ephesians 4:30—Paul said, "Grieve not the Holy Spirit, by whom ye are sealed."

b) 1 Thessalonians 5:19—Paul said, "Quench not the Spirit."

c) Galatians 2:20—Paul said, "I am crucified with Christ: nevertheless I live; yet not I, but Christ liveth in me." It is the Spirit of Christ who lives in all believers.

d) John 7:37-39—John said, "Jesus stood and cried out, saying, If any man thirst, let him come unto me, and drink. He that believeth on me, as the Scripture hath said, out of his heart shall flow rivers of living water.

But this spoke he of the Spirit, whom they that believe on him should receive." All who believe in Christ receive the Holy Spirit. The New Testament is unlike the Old in that David cried out, "Take not thy Holy Spirit from me" (Ps. 51:11). Ever since the Day of Pentecost, the Holy Spirit comes as a permanent resident to every believer.

Just as the believer is never commanded to be baptized by the Holy Spirit, neither is he commanded to be indwelt by the Spirit. Both are guaranteed for the person who places his faith in Christ for salvation. We are sealed by the Spirit (cf. Eph. 1:13). The command to be obeyed is to be filled, or controlled, by the Holy Spirit.

B. The Meaning of Being Filled with the Spirit

1. A continuous action

The Greek verb (a present passive imperative) for "be filled" in Ephesians 5:18 is literally translated "be being kept filled" (with the Spirit). The command is for continuous filling, or controlling, of the Spirit of God in the believer's life. Because the Greek verb is passive, it denotes that the believer is filled with the Spirit, not that he fills himself. The present active imperative would denote that. At salvation the believer is baptized by means of the Spirit into the Body of Christ, indwelt by the Spirit, and sealed by the Spirit unto the day of redemption. But a Christian can live a life of defeat if he does not enjoy the moment-by-moment experience of being continually filled by the Spirit of God.

2. A comparative analysis

The word *filled* brings to mind a glass filled with liquid or a box filled with some substance. But that is not the idea behind the Greek word translated "filled" (*plēroō*) in the New Testament.

a) Pressure

Plēroō was used often of the wind's filling a sail to move a ship along. To be filled with the Holy Spirit is to be moved along in our Christian life by God Himself, the same dynamic by which the writers of Scripture were "moved by the Holy Spirit" (2 Pet. 1:21). You don't move in your own energy or with your own ideas but are generated by the agency of the Spirit. To be filled with the Spirit is to be carried along on a moment-by-moment enterprise bent on accomplishing the will of God.

b) Permeation

Plēroō also carries the idea of permeation.

(1) The salt principle

The word was sometimes used of salt's permeating meat in order to flavor and preserve it. In the same way the Holy Spirit both preserves and flavors the Christian life. God wants His Holy Spirit to so permeate the lives of His children that everything they think, say, and do will reflect His divine presence.

(2) The Fizzie principle

Fizzies were popular in the early 1970s. They resembled Alka-Seltzer tablets and were used to make different flavored soft drinks. Dropped in a glass of water, the tablets permeated the water and transformed it into a flavored drink—for instance, a grape Fizzie produced a grape soda. The Spirit of God wants to so flavor the believer's life that he tastes exactly like the Spirit of God. When someone is around you he should feel as though he has been with Jesus because He permeates your life (cf. Acts 4:13).

(3) The control principle

However, *plēroō* was mainly used to get across the idea of total control. Whenever a gospel writer wanted to speak of someone who was dominated by his emotions, he used *plēroō*.

(a) In general

   i) John 16:6—Jesus said, "Because I have said these things unto you, sorrow hath filled your heart."

   ii) Luke 5:26—Luke said the people "were all amazed, and they glorified God, and were filled with fear."

   iii) Luke 6:11—Luke said the Jewish leaders "were filled with fury, and discussed one with another what they might do to Jesus."

A person who is filled in this sense is no longer under his own control but under the control of that which dominates him. The same thing is true in living the Christian life. To be filled with the Holy Spirit is not to have Him progressively added to our life but to be dominated by Him.

(b) In specific

   i) Jesus

      Matthew records that Jesus was led by the Spirit into the wilderness to be tested by the devil (Matt. 4:1). Luke clarifies that further by saying, "Jesus, being full of the Holy Spirit, returned from the Jordan, and was led by the Spirit into the wilderness" (Luke 4:1). Mark makes it even stronger: "The Spirit driveth [Gk., *ekballō*] him into the wilderness" (Mark 1:12). It's not that Jesus resisted or had to be coerced, because His greatest joy was to do His Father's will (cf. John 4:34). He submitted Himself entirely to the Spirit's control. Because He was full of the Holy Spirit, He was controlled by the Spirit. Likewise, if the Christian is not controlled and empowered by the Holy Spirit, he is of limited use to God.

A Christian can accomplish no more without being filled with the Holy Spirit than a glove can accomplish without being filled with a hand. Anything he manages to do is but wood, hay, and straw, which amounts to nothing and will eventually be burned (1 Cor. 3:12-15). Functioning in the flesh (apart from the Spirit) produces nothing of spiritual value. When the Lord wants a task accomplished, He will always use someone who is full of the Spirit.

ii) Stephen

When the church at Jerusalem wanted to free up the apostles for the more important work of prayer and ministering the Word, they chose men such as Stephen, who was "full of faith and of the Holy Spirit" (Acts 6:5). They chose Stephen because he was obviously controlled by the Holy Spirit. Acts 7:55 says that "he being full of the Holy Spirit, looked up steadfastly into heaven, and saw the glory of God, and Jesus standing on the right hand of God." That was when he was being stoned. As he lay on the ground beneath the Jewish leaders' feet, he had a view of God that was unlike anything he had ever seen before. Being filled with the Spirit takes you out of the human realm and fixes your eyes on the right perspective— God's glory and not your own. Being filled with the Spirit makes everything else of secondary importance—and often of no importance at all.

iii) Paul

When God needed a man to share His message of salvation to the Gentiles, He chose the apostle Paul, but not before He had Ananias lay hands on him and say, "The Lord, even Jesus, that appeared unto thee in the way as thou camest, hath sent me, that thou mightest receive thy sight, and be filled with the Holy Spirit" (Acts 9:17). Before Paul's ministry could begin, he had to be filled with the Spirit or his work would have been done in the flesh. Being filled with the Spirit is simply living one moment at a time under the complete control of the Holy Spirit. When God wants someone to minister in His church or to do pioneer missionary work, He always looks for someone filled with the Spirit.

C. The Means of Being Filled with the Spirit

Being filled with the Holy Spirit is not a prayer request. It is a command to be obeyed. And if God gives a command, the believer must have the resources to obey it.

1. Surrendering your life to Christ

Being filled with the Spirit involves surrendering one's will, intellect, emotions, as well as one's time, talent, and treasure to God's complete control. It is the death of self-will. When you are right with God and are filled with His Spirit, you will be right with everyone else. You will speak to others in psalms, hymns, and spiritual songs (Eph. 5:19), be thankful for all things (v. 20), and submit yourself to fellow believers (v. 21). Wives will submit to their husbands (vv. 22-24), husbands will love their wives as Christ loved the church (vv. 25-33), children will obey their parents (6:1-3), parents will not provoke their children to wrath (v. 4), servants will be obedient to their masters (vv. 5-8), and masters will treat their servants correctly (v. 9). Being filled with the Spirit results not in ecstatic experiences but in right relationships with God and man.

2. Studying the Word of Christ

Colossians 3:16-25 is the parallel passage to Ephesians 5:18–6:9. The Ephesians passage states that right relationships occur only when a believer is filled with the Spirit, whereas the Colossians passage states, "Let the word of Christ dwell in you richly, in all wisdom teaching and admonishing one another, in psalms and hymns and spiritual songs singing with grace in your hearts to the Lord. And whatever ye do in word or deed, do all in the name of the Lord Jesus, giving thanks to God and the Father by him" (vv. 16-17). Being filled with the Spirit then is simply letting the Word of Christ (Scripture) infuse every part of your being. To be filled with the Spirit is to be filled with God's Word. The two are synonymous.

If you want to be Spirit-filled, then feed yourself a steady diet of the Word of God. When you do, you will find yourself coming under the Spirit's control, because the Author of the Word of God is the Spirit of God. When the Word of God is received into the believer's life, the Spirit takes that truth and gives guidance and direction.

3. Standing in the presence of Christ

Peter always wanted to be near Jesus. When Jesus walked down the road, Peter was with Him. If the Lord went up on a mountain, Peter went with Him. When the Lord said, "Will ye also go away?" Peter responded, "Lord, to whom shall we go? Thou hast the words of eternal life" (John 6:67-68). Peter got into trouble only when he got away from the Lord. When he stayed close to Christ he said and did amazing things.

a) Peter before Pentecost

(1) Miraculous works

When Peter saw Jesus standing on the water, he wanted to be with Him. Matthew records that Peter said, "Lord, if it be thou, bid me come unto thee on the water. And he said, Come. And when Peter was come down out of the boat, he walked on the water, to go to Jesus" (Matt. 14:28-29). Peter was successful in his attempt to walk on water until his attention turned from Jesus to his circumstances.

(2) Miraculous words

Jesus asked His disciples, "Who do men say that I, the son of man, am?" (Matt. 16:13). Peter responded, "Thou art the Christ, the Son of the living God. And Jesus answered and said unto him, Blessed art thou, Simon Barjona; for flesh and blood hath not revealed it unto thee, but my Father, who is in heaven" (vv. 16-17). Peter's mouth was available, and God used it to reveal divine truth. A short while later however, Peter pitted his own understanding against the Lord's and discovered that he then spoke for Satan (Matt. 16:22-23).

(3) Miraculous courage

When the soldiers came to arrest Jesus in the Garden of Gethsemane, they fell to the ground when Jesus identified Himself as the One they were seeking. Taking courage in the presence of Jesus, Peter took out his sword and cut off the right ear of Malchus, a slave of the high priest. He probably would have fought to the death had not Jesus restrained him. While standing next to Jesus, Peter was ready to take on the Roman army—possibly as many as five hundred soldiers—single-handedly! Peter was able to do the miraculous because he was in the presence of Jesus Christ. No wonder he always wanted to be near Him. When Peter was near the Lord, he feared no one. But a short while later, when Christ was taken from him, he didn't have the courage even to admit knowing Him.

b) Peter after Pentecost

However, Peter's boldness was not limited to the earthly ministry of Jesus Christ. After the Lord ascended to heaven, He sent the Holy Spirit to indwell His disciples as He had promised (John 14:15-26; 16:12-15).

(1) Miraculous words

Peter stood before the enemies of Christ on the Day of Pentecost and said, "Ye men of Judaea, and all ye that dwell at Jerusalem, be this known unto you, and hearken to my words. . . . Now when they heard this, they were pricked in their heart. . . . The same day there were added unto them about three thousand souls" (Acts 2:14, 37, 41). Peter preached a masterful sermon as God used his mouth to bring thousands to Himself. Peter had the courage to fearlessly proclaim his risen Lord in the city where, a few weeks earlier, Jesus had been arrested, beaten, and crucified.

(2) Miraculous works

Peter and John, on their way to the Temple to worship, encountered a beggar who had been lame for forty years. The beggar asked Peter and John for money, but Peter replied, "Silver and gold have I none, but, such as I have, give I thee. In the name of Jesus Christ of Nazareth, rise up and walk. And he took him by the right hand, and lifted him up; and immediately his feet and ankle bones received strength. And he, leaping up, stood and walked, and entered with them

66

into the temple, walking, and leaping, and praising God" (Acts 3:6-8).

(3) Miraculous courage

Because of their continued preaching, Peter and John were taken before the Sanhedrin—the Jewish court—and told to stop. They responded, "Whether it is right in the sight of God to hearken unto you more than unto God, judge ye. For we cannot but speak the things which we have seen and heard" (Acts 4:19-20). The key to Peter's boldness was that he was "filled with the Holy Spirit" (Acts 2:4).

To be filled with the Spirit is to be conscious of the Lord's presence. For Peter, being filled with the Spirit was like walking next to Jesus!

Conclusion

When you surrender to the control of God's Spirit, you will find that God produces amazing things in your life, too. Paul calls those marvelous blessings "the fruit of the Spirit," and they are: "love, joy, peace, patience, kindness, goodness, faithfulness, gentleness, self-control" (Gal. 5:22-23, NASB). He continues, "If we live by the Spirit, let us also walk by the Spirit" (Gal. 5:24-25, NASB). To walk in the Spirit is to live to our potential as God's children.

Focusing on the Facts

1. The key to rightly living the Christian life is being _____ by the Holy Spirit (see p. 54).
2. What are two opposite interpretations of being filled with the Spirit (see p. 54)?
3. True or false: No Christian can fulfill God's will for his life apart from being filled with His Spirit (see p. 55).
4. Can you be a Christian and not be habitually obedient to God? Explain your answer (see p. 55).

5. To what do the words *carnal* and *fleshly* predominately refer (see p. 56)?
6. What was Paul saying in 1 Corinthians 3 about "carnal" Christians (see p. 56)?
7. Does every Christian possess the Holy Spirit in all His fullness? Explain your answer (see p. 57).
8. What does it mean to be baptized with the Holy Spirit (see pp. 57-58)?
9. Are all Christians indwelt by the Holy Spirit at all times? If so, why do they need to be filled with the Holy Spirit (see pp. 58-59)?
10. What are the different ways the word translated "filled" is used in Scripture? What is the dominant thought in the different usages (see pp. 59-60)?
11. Give specific examples of people in the Bible who were filled with the Spirit (see pp. 61-63).
12. Being filled with the Holy Spirit is not a _____ _____. It is a _____ (see p. 63).
13. What are the means for being filled with the Spirit (see pp. 63-64)?
14. True or false: Being filled with the Spirit means the death of self-will (see p. 63).
15. What is the result of being filled with the Spirit? What happens to your relationship with others (see pp. 63-64)?
16. How does Colossians 3:16-25, a parallel passage to Ephesians 5:18–6:9, help us to understand what being filled with the Spirit means (see p. 64)?
17. If you want to be Spirit-filled, then feed yourself a steady diet of the _____ of _____ (see p. 64).
18. To be filled with the Spirit is to be _____ of the Lord's _____ (see p. 67).
19. By examining the life of Peter, what can we conclude being filled with the Spirit is like (see pp. 65-67)?
20. How is being filled with the Spirit related to the fruit of the Spirit (see p. 67)?

Pondering the Principles

1. There is much confusion today concerning those who claim to be Christians and yet are not obedient to God on a continuing

basis. First John cuts through the confusion by declaring that if a person's life is not characterized by righteous living, he is not a Christian. Are you truly saved? Is the pattern of your life one of continual obedience? Read the book of 1 John one chapter a day for the next five days, and ask God to confirm in your heart whether you are truly saved.

2. As believers are called to be filled with the Spirit in Ephesians 5:18, they are also called to exhibit the fruit of the Spirit in Galatians 5:22-23. Do you exhibit the fruit of the Spirit in your life? Is it apparent to others around you that you are a Christian and controlled by the Spirit of God? After your study of 1 John, take each aspect of the fruit of the Spirit, and examine your own heart over the next two weeks to determine if you are truly living in the Spirit.

5
Be Filled with the Spirit—Part 2

Outline

Introduction
A. Christ-Consciousness
B. Christlikeness

Review
I. The Contrast (v. 18*a*)
II. The Command (v. 18*b*)
   A. The Misconceptions of Being Filled with the Spirit
   B. The Meaning of Being Filled with the Spirit
   C. The Means of Being Filled with the Spirit

Lesson
   D. The Metaphor of Being Filled with the Spirit
      1. The problem
      2. The pitfall
         a) The characteristics of the flesh
         b) The chastening of God
      3. The potential
         a) The specifics
         b) The summary
III. The Consequences (vv. 19-21)
   A. The Inward Result—Singing (v. 19)
      1. The cause
         a) Colossians 3:16
         b) James 5:13
      2. The character
      3. The connection
      4. The choristers
         a) In the Old Testament
         b) In the New Testament

Questions for Singing Saints
Question 1: To Whom Do We Sing?
Question 2: Where Do Our Songs Originate?
    A. The Sound of Music
    B. The Significance of Music
    C. The Style of Music

Introduction

A. Christ-Consciousness

Living in the Spirit means living every moment as if you were actually standing in the presence of Christ. Having your thoughts controlled by Christ is the heart of the Spirit-filled life. God is not necessarily interested in future commitments. If a man's wife came to him and said, "Honey, do you love me?" he wouldn't respond by saying, "Why don't you check with me in a few weeks?" She's not interested in finding out in a few weeks. She wants to know now. God is the same way. He is wholly interested in what a Christian's life is like in the present. A believer's life is to be controlled by the Holy Spirit from beginning to end with no gaps in between.

Realize that you can never live your life in the future. When the future arrives, it is no longer the future but the present. Likewise you can never live in the past. You will always be in the present, and it is the only moment that matters. Being filled with the Spirit means filling your life with the Word of God so that your thoughts are dominated by Christ.

B. Christlikeness

The apostle Paul described a wonderful by-product of being filled with the Spirit: "We all, with unveiled face beholding as in a mirror the glory of the Lord, are changed into the same image from glory to glory, even as by the Spirit of the Lord" (2 Cor. 3:18). As you gaze at the glory of the Lord, which means to focus solely on Christ, you will be changed into His image by the Holy Spirit. Christ-consciousness leads to Christlikeness. As you are filled with the Holy Spirit you become increasingly more like Christ.

When you function in your own flesh, apart from the Holy Spirit, there will be no progress or maturity in your Christian life. The key to living the Christian life is to move toward Christlikeness as you are filled with the Holy Spirit. That is the only way a believer can experience true joy and victory.

Review

I. THE CONTRAST (v. 18*a*; see pp. 7-17)

II. THE COMMAND (v. 18*b*)

   A. The Misconceptions of Being Filled with the Spirit (see pp. 55-59)

   B. The Meaning of Being Filled with the Spirit (see pp. 59-63)

   C. The Means of Being Filled with the Spirit (see pp. 63-67)

Lesson

   D. The Metaphor of Being Filled with the Spirit

   The filling of the Spirit is well illustrated by the metaphor of walking in Galatians 5:16-26. All you need to do in the Christian life is to take one step at a time. Paul begins by saying, "Walk in the Spirit and ye shall not fulfill the lust of the flesh" (v. 16). The Greek construction of the verse literally means, "Keep on walking in the Spirit."

   1. The problem

      The believer's only resource to override his evil desires and the temptations of Satan is to continue walking in the Spirit. I've heard so many people say, "The devil and his demons are after me! I must get someone to get rid of the demons." The real issue is probably not the influence of Satan in their lives as much as an unwillingness to walk daily in the Spirit.

2. The pitfall

There is a war going on inside the believer. Paul explains, "The flesh lusteth against the Spirit, and the Spirit against the flesh; and these are contrary the one to the other" (v. 17). The believer's flesh is the beachhead of sin. That's where Satan lands with his guns of temptation. Even though believers are new creatures in Christ (2 Cor. 5:17), there is still the inevitability of sin. Paul recognizes that element of human nature in Rom. 7:15-17: "That which I am doing, I do not understand; for I am not practicing what I would like to do, but I am doing the very thing I hate. But if I do the very thing I do not wish to do, I agree with the Law, confessing that it is good. So now, no longer am I the one doing it, but sin which indwells me" (NASB).

a) The characteristics of the flesh

The results of living in the flesh are devastating: "adultery, fornication, uncleanness, lasciviousness, idolatry, sorcery, hatred, strife, jealousy, wrath, factions, seditions, heresies, envyings, murders, drunkenness, revelings, and the like . . . they who do such things shall not inherit the kingdom of God" (Gal. 5:19-21). People whose lives are characterized by the works of the flesh are definitely not Christians.

b) The chastening of God

When you walk in the flesh, you exhibit the characteristics of unbelievers and fall into God's chastening. Paul says, "If ye be led by the Spirit, ye are not under the law" (v. 18). The opposite is also true. If you are not walking in the Spirit, you are in danger of not being saved at all and therefore falling under the judgment of God's law. And God will deal out terrible retribution (2 Thess. 1:8). However, if you continue to walk in the Spirit, you give evidence of true saving faith and escape the chastening hand of God. You must make the choice, and if you choose to follow the flesh, you must also face the consequences.

3. The potential

The best way to deal with the lust of the flesh is simply to walk in the Spirit. If you are controlled by the Spirit of God and are Christ-conscious on a daily basis because you are feeding on His Word, you are not going to have a problem with the flesh. Your mind cannot be occupied with two masters at the same time. You cannot be concentrating on Jesus Christ and at the same time concentrating on the lusts of your own flesh. You have to dispel the lust of the flesh in order for the Holy Spirit to control your life. Those who give in to the flesh take the path of least resistance. We must study the Scriptures and spend time in prayer, or there will be an unwillingness to walk in the Spirit.

a) The specifics

Paul says in Galatians 5:22-24, "The fruit of the Spirit is love, joy, peace, long-suffering, gentleness, goodness, faith, meekness, self-control; against such things there is no law. And they that are Christ's have crucified the flesh with the affections and lusts." If you yield to the control of the Spirit, the fruit of the Spirit will be produced and obedience will characterize your life. You will never fall under the condemnation of God's law because there is no penalty for righteous living. If you desire to live a happy, peaceful, and meaningful life, walk in the Spirit.

b) The summary

Paul sums everything up in verse 25: "If we live in the Spirit [positionally], let us also walk in the Spirit [practically]." His argument in effect is, "What's the sense of living in the Spirit and walking in the flesh? If you've begun in the Spirit, and live in the Spirit, then walk daily in the Spirit!" God desires all His children to reach their potential, bringing glory to

Him by their obedience and fruitfulness. Paul is communicating the same thing in both Ephesians 5 and Galatians 5. Living in the Spirit, walking in the Spirit, and being filled with the Spirit are all saying the same thing: God wants believers to be controlled by Him, not by themselves.

III. THE CONSEQUENCES (vv. 19-21)

"Speaking to yourselves in psalms and hymns and spiritual songs, singing and making melody in your heart to the Lord, giving thanks always for all things unto God and the Father in the name of our Lord Jesus Christ, submitting yourselves one to another in the fear of God."

These are the results or consequences of being filled with the Spirit: singing, saying thanks, and submission. When God's Spirit controls us, He puts a song in our hearts and on our lips, give us a thankful spirit, and makes us willing to carry out the wishes of others. The first is inward, the second upward, and the third outward. The filling of the Holy Spirit makes us rightly related to ourselves, to God, and to others.

A. The Inward Result—Singing (v. 19)

"Speaking to yourselves in psalms and hymns and spiritual songs, singing and making melody in your heart to the Lord."

The Spirit-filled life produces music. Whether he has a good voice or cannot carry a tune, the Spirit-filled Christian is a singing Christian. Nothing is more indicative of a fulfilled life, a contented soul, and a happy heart than the expression of song. You would think the first result of responding to a tremendous theological truth like "be filled with the Spirit" would be to have faith that moves mountains, ecstatic spiritual experiences, or dynamic preaching ability. But the first result of being Spirit-filled is simply a joyful heart that wants to sing.

1. The cause

Singing is an expression of the emotion of the soul. If there is anything that ought to be different about Christians, it ought to be their music. Since music is the language of the soul, then the believer's music ought to be different from that of the world's.

a) Colossians 3:16—Paul said, "Let the word of Christ dwell in you richly, in all wisdom teaching and admonishing one another, in psalms and hymns and spiritual songs singing with grace in your hearts to the Lord." Spirit-filled singing always starts from the heart and is directed to the Lord.

b) James 5:13—James said, "Is any among you afflicted? Let him pray. Is any merry? Let him sing psalms." Singing is an expression of the joy of the Holy Spirit. Redemption gives man a new song.

2. The character

The word *new* is used in the Bible more times in relation to song than to any other feature of salvation. As new creatures in Christ we have a new nature, a new life, a new birth, and a new song. When God redeems men, He gives them a distinctive song, more beautiful and pure than anything the world can produce. It is not a new in terms of chronology but in character and quality.

3. The connection

Every time the phrase "a new song" is mentioned in Scripture, it is connected with salvation. Salvation always produces a new song in the redeemed.

a) Psalm 33:1-5—The psalmist said, "Rejoice in the Lord, O ye righteous; for praise is befitting to the upright. Praise the Lord with the harp; sing unto him with the psaltery and an instrument of ten strings. Sing unto him a new song; play skillfully with a loud noise. For the word of the Lord is right, and all his works are done in truth. He loveth righteousness and justice; the earth is full of the goodness of the Lord."

b) Psalm 40:2-3—David said, "He brought me up also out of an horrible pit, out of the miry clay, and set my feet upon a rock, and established my goings. And he hath put a new song in my mouth."

c) Psalm 96:1-2—The psalmist said, "Oh, sing unto the Lord a new song; sing unto the Lord, all the earth. Sing unto the Lord, bless his name; show forth his salvation from day to day."

d) Psalm 98:1-2—The psalmist said, "Oh, sing unto the Lord a new song; for he hath done marvelous things; his right hand, and his holy arm, have gotten him the victory. The Lord hath made known his salvation."

e) Psalm 144:9—David said, "I will sing a new song unto thee."

f) Psalm 149:1—The psalmist said, "Sing unto the Lord a new song."

g) Revelation 5:9—John observed the four living creatures and the twenty-four elders singing "a new song, saying, Thou [the Lamb—Jesus Christ] art worthy to take the scroll, and to open its seals; for thou wast slain, and hast redeemed us to God by thy blood out of every kindred, and tongue, and people, and nation." This is one of the two places in the book of Revelation where angels are said to be singing.

The first angelic choir sang when God created the earth, for then the "morning stars [angels] sang together" (Job 38:7). That was before the fall of man. The next time we see them singing is when Jesus Christ comes to set up His kingdom and regain paradise. The angels won't sing in the meantime because the new song is the song of the redeemed, and angels don't experience redemption. They sing at the end because of the redemption of creation.

h) Exodus 15:1-2—Moses, in his song of redemption, said, "I will sing unto the Lord, for he hath triumphed gloriously: the horse and his rider hath he thrown into the sea. The Lord is my strength and song, and he is become my salvation; he is my God, and I will prepare him an habitation; my father's God, and I will exalt him." After he finished singing, Moses' sister, Miriam, led the women in further singing and dancing (vv. 20-21).

    i) Judges 5:2-3—When the Lord delivered Israel from the Canaanites, Deborah and Barak sang, "Praise ye the Lord for the avenging of Israel, when the people willingly offered themselves. Hear, O ye kings; give ear, O ye princes; I even I, will sing unto the Lord; I will sing praise to the Lord God of Israel." That is the first duet recorded in Scripture, and it was a duet of redemption explaining how God had spared His people.

4. The choristers

    a) In the Old Testament

        (1) 1 Chronicles 23:5—David said, "Four thousand praised the Lord with the instruments which I made."

        (2) 1 Samuel 10:5—Samuel said to Saul, "Thou shalt come to the hill of God, where is the garrison of the Philistines; and it shall come to pass, when thou art come there to the city, that thou shalt meet a company of prophets coming down from the high place with a psaltery, and a timbrel, and a flute, and a harp before them."

        (3) 1 Chronicles 13:8—"David and all Israel played before God with all their might, and with singing, and with harps, and with psalteries, and with timbrels, and with cymbals, and with trumpets." Praise is fitting to God.

        (4) 1 Chronicles 16:4-6—David "appointed certain of the Levites to minister before the ark of the Lord . . . with psalteries and with harps . . . with cymbals . . . with trumpets continually before the the ark of the covenant of God."

(5) Ezra 2:65—Ezra records that Governor Zerubbabel had "two hundred singing men and singing women."

(6) Nehemiah 12:40-43—"So stood the two companies of them who gave thanks in the house of God . . . with trumpets . . . and the singers sang loud . . . and rejoiced; for God had made them rejoice with great joy. And the women and the children rejoiced, so that the joy of Jerusalem was heard even afar off." This is what is known as antiphonal singing—different groups singing alternately.

(7) Ezekiel 40:44-47—"Outside the inner gate were the chambers of the singers in the inner court" (v. 44). When Jesus ultimately returns to set up His millennial kingdom, the curse of man will be reversed and the angels will sing again. One of the first things He will do is construct a Temple. Within that Temple will be a huge choir loft for singing to the glory of God.

b) In the New Testament

(1) Matthew 26:30—Matthew records that right after the Last Supper, "when they had sung an hymn, they went out into the Mount of Olives." The disciples got together with Jesus and sang before the crucifixion.

(2) Acts 4:24—Luke said the early church "lifted up their voice to God with one accord." Acts 4:24-30 records what may be one of the first hymns of the early church.

(3) Acts 16:25—While in prison for their faith, Paul and Silas "prayed, and sang praises unto God."

(4) 1 Corinthians 14:15—In trying to correct the singing of the Corinthians Paul said, "I will sing with the Spirit, and I will sing with the understanding also." There has always been music with God's people.

(5) Revelation 14:2-3—John said, "I heard a voice from heaven, like the voice of many waters, and like the voice of a great thunder; and I heard the voice of harpers harping with their harps. And they sang, as it were, a new song before the throne, and before the four living creatures and the elders; and no man could learn that song but the hundred and forty and four thousand, who were redeemed from the earth." In the future will be a 144,000-voice choir with heavenly harpists for accompaniment.

(6) Revelation 15:2-3—John recorded that those who will be victorious over the Beast (the Antichrist) have "the harps of God. And they sing the song of Moses, the servant of God, and the song of the Lamb." God loves music, both instrumental and vocal, that rightly reflects His glory.

Questions for Singing Saints

QUESTION 1: To Whom Do We Sing?

"Speaking to yourselves."

The primary audience for our singing is fellow believers and ultimately the Lord. Music is never characterized in the Bible as being evangelistic, although God may use the gospel content set to music to bring truth to the lost and thus lead them to Himself. Since the gospel message is so powerful, the open heart may receive it even though it comes with a melody, but that is not the original intent for music.

Songs without a clear or complete presentation of God's truth can be counterproductive by producing a feeling of well-being and contentment that is counterfeit to God's peace and that serves to further insulate an unbeliever from the true, saving gospel. It is unfortunate when some well-meaning singers put their songs into the world's vernacular and dilute the message. What is meant to be evangelistic turns out to be only a watered-down message that saves no one. God's primary design

81

for music is as the expression of a life controlled by the Holy Spirit. Music is to be used in corporate and individual worship.

QUESTION 2: Where Do Our Songs Originate?

"In your heart."

The heart makes the voice sing, and God's Spirit is what prompts the heart. If the heart isn't right, however, there will be no song (cf. Ps. 137:1-4). God isn't interested in songs from an unclean heart (Amos 5:23-24). Many sing for money and recognition but not from a Spirit-controlled heart. Those are not the songs the Lord wants to hear. If you have an opportunity to sing a solo or play an instrument, but your heart is not filled with the Spirit of God, don't sing or play at all. The song of the redeemed is the new song of men and women controlled by the Spirit of God. God has given music a high priority because it is an expression of worship. Sacred music is totally different from secular music because the Spirit of God is unique.

A. The Sound of Music

Those who don't know God have tried to come up with their own music, but it only mirrors their evil. The pulsating rhythms of some native African music mimics the restless, superstitious passions of their culture and pagan religion. Much of the music in the Orient is dissonant and unresolved, going from nowhere to nowhere, with no beginning and no end—just as their religions go from cycle to cycle in endless repetitions of meaningless existence. Their music, like their destiny, is without resolution.

The music of much of the Western world is seductive and suggestive, reflecting the immoral, lustful society that produces, sings, and enjoys it. And a good percentage of rock music, with its bombastic atonality and dissonance, mirrors people who reject both God and reason and float without orientation in a sea of relativity and unrestrained self-expression.

B. The Significance of Music

Many of the physical and emotional effects of modern music have allegedly been demonstrated scientifically. Howard Hanson, director of the Eastman School of Music at the University of Rochester, has stated that "music can be soothing or invigorating, ennobling or vulgarizing, philosophical or orgiastic. It has the powers for evil as well as for good" (*The American Journal of Psychiatry*, vol. 99, p. 317).

I remember reading several years ago about a study on the effects of music on plants. Steve Lawhead's *Rock Reconsidered* (Downer's Grove, Ill.: InterVarsity, 1981) describes how this famous experiment was supposedly carried out on three groups of plants: "The plants in plot A got good healthy doses of classical music beamed at them all day long. Plant plot B was strafed relentlessly with hard rock. Plant plot C was a control group that heard only the sounds of mother nature herself. The results? Plot A developed a strong affinity for classical music and grew in the direction of the speakers. Plot C grew straight and tall as average plants do. But plot B, subjected to hard rock, first turned away from the speakers and then sickened and died" (p. 63).

Whether rock music therefore has the ability to damage the human body or not, things of infinitely greater value have the potential of being destroyed—the hearts and souls of men and women who allow Satan an open door because of where they put their affections. The Greek philosopher Aristotle wisely observed that music represents the passions of the soul, and if one listens to the wrong music he will become the wrong kind of person (*Problemata* 19).

C. The Style of Music

It is important to remember that it is impossible to generalize about a certain style of music. Primarily what the music communicates determines if it is evil. If a song advocates an ungodly life-style, then it would be wrong to allow its message to shape your thinking. A Christian message might be communicated in a rock style, and an ungodly message might be communicated in a musical style that is more restrained. A particular style of music isn't automatically right or wrong. There are several principles to consider when selecting a style of music to listen to:

1. What is the lyrical content of the song? Are the words true? Do they paint a biblical picture of life or a distorted one?

2. Is the singer or songwriter's life characterized by flagrant opposition to God and His standards? If so, don't support such people by purchasing their recordings or programming your mind with their ungodliness.

3. Does the song draw you closer to the Lord or away from Him? Does it wake sinful thoughts or actions in you? Does it make you conscious of the Savior or only of the singer?

Scripture's admonition that "all things be done properly and in an orderly manner" (1 Cor. 14:40, NASB) applies to music as well as to everything else. The book of Proverbs says to "keep thy heart with all diligence; for out of it [flow] the issues of life" (4:23). Philippians 4:8 is helpful to keep in mind when determining the value of any musical piece: "Whatever is true, whatever is honorable, whatever is right, whatever is pure, whatever is lovely, whatever is of good repute, if there is any excellence and if anything worthy of praise, let your mind dwell on these things" (NASB).

Focusing on the Facts

1. Living in the Spirit means living every moment as if you were standing in the _____ of Jesus Christ (see p. 72).

2. True or false: Being filled with the Spirit means filling your life with the Word of God so that your thoughts are dominated by Christ (see p. 72).
3. What is the key to living the Christian life (see p. 73)?
4. How does Galatians 5:16-26 illustrate living in the Spirit (see p. 73)?
5. The believer's flesh is the _____ of sin (see p. 74).
6. What are the results of living in the flesh? What can we conclude about those whose lives are characterized by the works of the flesh (see p. 74)?
7. What is the best way to deal with the lust of the flesh (see p. 75)?
8. What must we do to avoid giving in to the flesh (see p. 75)?
9. What is the inward result of being filled with the Spirit (see p. 76)?
10. True or false: Nothing is more indicative of a fulfilled life, a contented soul, and a happy heart than the expression of song (see p. 76).
11. If there is anything that ought to be different about Christians, it ought to be their _____ (see pp. 76-77).
12. What is characteristic of the phrase "a new song" in Scripture (see pp. 77-79)?
13. Who is the primary audience for singing saints? How is music to be used (see p. 81)?
14. Where does the music of the believer originate? Explain your answer (see p. 82).
15. What principles can be used to evaluate certain styles of music (see pp. 83-84)?
16. What verse in Philippians helps in determining the value of a particular piece of music (see p. 84)?

Pondering the Principles

1. The best way to fight sin is to be controlled by the Holy Spirit on a daily basis. That involves a moment-by-moment walk with Christ. The apostle Paul said, "This I say then, Walk in the Spirit, and ye shall not fulfill the lust of the flesh" (Gal. 5:16). Are you endeavoring on a daily basis to be controlled by the Spirit of God? Do you truly hate sin and its effects? If not,

confess your attitude to God, and ask Him to cause you to walk daily in the Spirit.

2. Do you listen to music? Why or why not? What type or style of music do you listen to? Why? As was mentioned in the chapter, there are several principles to consider when selecting a certain style of music. Reread those principles, and then evaluate the music you listen to. Finish your study by memorizing Philippians 4:8, and begin to evaluate all your future musical tastes in light of that verse.

6
Be Filled with the Spirit—Part 3

Outline

Introduction
A. The Believer's Inheritance
   1. The promise
   2. The proof
B. The Believer's Works
   1. The promise
   2. The proof
C. The Believer's Prayers
   1. The promise
   2. The proof
D. The Believer's Indwelling
   1. The promise
   2. The proof
E. The Believer's Fruit
   1. The promise
   2. The proof

Review
 I. The Contrast (v. 18a)
 II. The Command (v. 18b)
III. The Consequences (vv. 19-21)
     A. The Inward Result—Singing (v. 19)

Questions for Singing Saints
Question 1: To Whom Do We Sing?
Question 2: Where Do Our Songs Originate?

Lesson
Question 3: To Whom Do Believers Sing?
A. The Primary Object of Music
    1. 2 Chronicles 5:12-14
    2. Revelation 5:9, 11-13
B. The Profitable Effects of Music
    1. Mentally
    2. Physically
    3. Spiritually
Question 4: How Do Believers Sing?
A. The General Statement
    1. Revelation 4:1
    2. Revelation 10:4
B. The Specific Statements
    1. Singing songs
    2. Making melody
Question 5: In What Ways Should We Sing?
A. Psalms
B. Hymns
C. Spiritual Songs

Conclusion

Introduction

During Jesus' final night with His disciples, which is recorded in John 13-16, He promised them many wonderful things. The key to them all was the coming of the Holy Spirit. Jesus said, "I will pray the Father, and he shall give you another Comforter, that he may abide with you forever; even the Spirit of truth, whom the world cannot receive, because it seeth him not, neither knoweth him: but ye know him; for he dwelleth with you, and shall be in you" (John 14:16-17).

God often made promises through Christ that are confirmed by the Holy Spirit. That is the mystery of the triune Godhead. The Shema of the Old Testament declares, "Hear, O Israel: The Lord our God is one Lord" (Deut. 6:4). Scripture affirms there is only one God, yet it also declares that He is manifest in three distinct Persons: God the Father, God the Son, and God the Holy Spirit. It is the coming of God the Holy Spirit to permanently indwell believers that makes Christ's promises a reality.

A. The Believer's Inheritance

1. The promise

Jesus promised His children a heavenly inheritance, saying, "Let not your heart be troubled; ye believe in God, believe also in me. In my Father's house are many mansions; if it were not so, I would have told you. I go to prepare a place for you. And if I go and prepare a place for you, I will come again, and receive you unto myself, that where I am, there ye may be also" (John 14:1-3). Jesus was leaving His disciples and didn't want to leave them in a fearful state.

He went on to say, "The Spirit of truth, whom the world cannot receive, because it seeth him not, neither knoweth him: but ye know him; for he dwelleth with you, and shall be in you" (v. 17). God's design for the New Testament era is not that the Holy Spirit would just be alongside or with His people, as in Old Testament times, but that He would actually be in them forever.

2. The proof

A verification of Jesus' promise is recorded in Ephesians 1:13. Paul declared that in Christ, "in whom ye also trusted, after ye heard the word of truth, the gospel of your salvation; in whom also after ye believed, ye were sealed with that Holy Spirit of promise." The Greek word for "sealed" is *arrabōn*, which means "guarantee," "first installment," "down payment," or "engagement ring." The indwelling Holy Spirit is the believer's guarantee of a future heavenly inheritance. Christ was saying in John 14, "I am going to take those who believe in Me to heaven, and My down payment is the Holy Spirit."

B. The Believer's Works

1. The promise

Jesus not only promised the indwelling and guarantee of the Holy Spirit but also that His children would do even greater works in terms of extent and breadth than He did on earth. He said, "Verily, verily, I say unto you, He that believeth on me, the works that I do shall he do also; and greater works than these shall he do, because I go unto my Father" (John 14:12).

2. The proof

Jesus' ministry was confined to a local area. Believers, however, in the power of the Holy Spirit, multiply Jesus' ministry all over the world in His absence. Jesus said, "Ye shall receive power, after the Holy Spirit is come upon you; and ye shall be witnesses unto me both in Jerusalem, and in all Judaea, and in Samaria, and unto the uttermost part of the earth" (Acts 1:8).

C. The Believer's Prayers

1. The promise

Jesus also promised that He would answer the prayers of His own, saying, "Whatever ye shall ask in my name, that will I do, that the Father may be glorified in the Son. If ye shall ask anything in my name, I will do it" (John 14:13-14).

2. The proof

The fulfillment of Jesus' promise is the intercession of the Holy Spirit in the believer's life. Paul said, "The Spirit also helpeth our infirmity; for we know not what we should pray for as we ought; but the Spirit himself maketh intercession for us with groanings which cannot be uttered" (Rom. 8:26). The Holy Spirit continually intercedes on our behalf before the throne of God.

D. The Believer's Indwelling

1. The promise

Jesus promised that even though He had finished His earthly ministry, He would come back and indwell the believer in the Person of the Holy Spirit. He said, "I will not leave you comfortless; I will come to you. Yet a little while, and the world seeth me no more; but ye see me. Because I live, ye shall live also. At that day ye shall know that I am in my Father, and ye in me, and I in you" (John 14:18-20).

2. The proof

The fulfillment of that promise occurred on the Day of Pentecost. Luke records, "They were all filled with the Holy Spirit" (Acts 2:4). The Spirit of God now dwells in every believer.

E. The Believer's Fruit

1. The promise

Jesus also promised that when He finished His earthly ministry, He would not leave His children without peace. He said, "Peace I leave with you, my peace I give unto you; not as the world giveth, give I unto you. Let not your heart be troubled, neither let it be afraid" (John 14:27). Jesus not only promised peace but also joy: "These things have I spoken unto you, that my joy might remain in you" (John 15:11). He also wanted His disciples to experience love. Jesus said, "A new commandment I give unto you, that ye love one another; as I have loved you, that ye also love one another. By this shall all men know that ye are my disciples, if ye have love one to another" (John 13:34-35). In all Jesus promised love, joy, and peace to those who trusted in Him.

2. The proof

We find the fulfillment of that promise in Galatians 5:22: "The fruit of the Spirit is love, joy, peace."

The Holy Spirit is the channel through which the promises of Christ are fulfilled. The Lord Himself said, "He [the Holy Spirit] shall glorify me; for he shall receive of mine, and shall show it unto you" (John 16:14). If it were not for the indwelling Spirit in the believer, the promises of Christ could not be fulfilled in his life.

Even though every believer possesses all the promises of Christ, you will never be able to appropriate them unless you are filled by the Holy Spirit. Promises unfulfilled in the life of a believer are the equivalent of promises unmade. You will never realize what it is to have security in life and death, answered prayer, love, joy, and peace unless you are controlled by the Holy Spirit. That is the context of the text we are about to study.

Review

I. THE CONTRAST (v. 18a; see pp. 7-17)

II. THE COMMAND (v. 18b; see pp. 55-67, 73-76)

III. THE CONSEQUENCES (vv. 19-21)

    A. The Inward Result—Singing (v. 19; see pp. 76-81)

QUESTIONS FOR SINGING SAINTS

QUESTION 1: To Whom Do We Sing? (see pp. 81-82)

QUESTION 2: Where Do Our Songs Originate? (see pp. 82-84)

Lesson

QUESTION 3: To Whom Do Believers Sing?

"To the Lord."

A. The Primary Object of Music

    1. 2 Chronicles 5:12-14—"The Levites who were the singers, all of them of Asaph, of Heman, of Jeduthun, with their sons and their brethren, being arrayed in white linen, having cymbals and psalteries and harps, stood at the east end of the altar, and with them an hundred and twenty priests sounding with trumpets; It came even to pass, as the trumpeters and singers were

as one, to make one sound to be heard in praising and thanking the Lord; and when they lifted up their voice with the trumpets and cymbals and instruments of music, and praised the Lord, saying, For he is good; for his mercy endureth forever—that then the house was filled with a cloud, even the house of the Lord. So that the priests could not stand to minister by reason of the cloud; for the glory of the Lord had filled the house of God."

When the great Temple had been built, it was a glorious day in Israel. The Levites and other priests combined for a massive choir accompanied by 120 trumpets! God was so pleased with their worship that His Shekinah glory came down and filled the Temple in such a way that the priests could not minister. All God's people should desire to make themselves heard with one voice to praise and glorify the Lord.

2. Revelation 5:9, 11-13—The apostle John said, "They [saints] sang a new song, saying, Thou art worthy to take the scroll, and to open its seals; for thou wast slain, and hast redeemed us to God by thy blood out of every kindred, and tongue, and people, and nation. . . . And I beheld, and I heard the voice of many angels round about the throne and the living creatures and the elders, and the number of them was ten thousand times ten thousand, and thousands of thousands, saying with a loud voice, Worthy is the lamb that was slain to receive power, and riches, and wisdom, and strength, and honor, and glory, and blessing. And every creature that is in heaven, and on the earth, and under the earth, and such as are in the sea, and all that are in them, heard I saying, Blessing, and honor, and glory, and power be unto him that sitteth upon the throne, and unto the Lamb forever and ever." This is the great choir in the future that will sing to the Lord.

All music is be to offered to God. Johann Sebastian Bach, perhaps the greatest musician of all time, said that the aim of all music is the glory of God. In his own life and work the great composer and organist sought to live out that aim, frequently initialing his works S.D.G.: *Sola Deo Gloria*—to the glory of God alone.

Whenever believers sing, they must constantly remind themselves that their song should be a gift of praise to the Lord. Every word of every song should be biblical, rightly reflecting God's own thoughts and attitudes. It is tragic that much of the music today classified as Christian is nothing more than theological mishmash. It often reflects more of the world's philosophy than God's written revelation. It ought to be clear that Christian music is offered as praise to God.

B. The Profitable Effects of Music

As one filled with the Spirit offers music to God, it also blesses others. If at times I become depressed, I listen to praise music, and it rejuvenates my spirit. I begin to lift my heart toward God in praise and thanksgiving for what He has done in my life. A beautiful, soothing piece of music can calm nerves, remove fear and anxiety, reduce bitterness and anger, and help turn our attention from ourselves and our problems to God.

King David was a great musician, skillful singer, and a great writer of hymns. Many of the psalms are attributed to him. Whenever King Saul was troubled, he would call upon David to come and play for him. First Samuel 16:23 says, "When the evil spirit from God was upon Saul . . . David took an harp, and played with his hand; so Saul was refreshed, and was well, and the evil spirit departed from him." As David played his harp, Saul experienced three specific benefits: (1) he was refreshed (mental), (2) he was made well (physical), and (3) the evil spirit departed from him (spiritual).

1. Mentally

King Saul was in a time of tremendous anxiety, yet David's godly music refreshed his troubled mind. Seventeenth- and eighteenth-century physicians often prescribed music for mentally disturbed patients. They even recommended certain types of music to treat certain types of disorders. Music, as William Congreve said in *The Mourning Bride*, "has charms to soothe a savage breast."

Working from a more scientific basis, modern behaviorists have proved those ideas to be sound. Have you ever wondered why you choose one dentist over another? It may not be his drill or smile but his music. Studies have been done on what kind of music makes a person relaxed in the dentist's chair, what helps production in an office or assembly plant, and what kind of music helps reduce impatience in an elevator. Music has an ability to induce a quietness of mind.

The president of Musak Corporation has noted that, unlike drugs, music affects us psychologically and physiologically without invading the blood stream. Research has indicated the inherent quality of music to influence our metabolism, our heartbeat, and our pulse. He claims that Musak Corporation has made a unique specialization in nonentertainment applications of music as it relates to behavioral sciences. The subtle influence of music has been harnessed in programs providing a controlled stimulus for people at work. Music indeed affects our thinking. It is not possible to submit the spiritual effects of music to scientific testing, but it is reasonable to assume that music focusing the heart on God can help heal the spiritual ills of His people.

2. Physically

Seventeenth-century German Jesuit scholar Anastasias Kircher devoted a section of his book dealing with all forms of magnetism to the powerful magnetism of music. He discovered that music causes a reverberation of the air around the body and can cause a variation in the flow of bodily fluids whether it be blood, saliva, or lymphatic fluid. Kircher writes that a song entitled "Tarantella" was actually written to extract the poison from someone bitten by a tarantula! The famous dance by the same name accompanies it.

Music is used in many hospitals as an aid to health (note for example *Music in Hospitals*, by Willem van de Wall [New York: Russell Sage Foundation, 1946]). Sometimes patients in rooms with music recovered faster than patients having the same basic ailment who were in rooms without music.

There is a certain kind of musical rhythm known as "stopped anapestic" that is known to reduce physical strength. It is composed of two short beats, a long beat, and then a pause—opposite the human heartbeat. Music has the potential for making a profound effect on the human body.

3. Spiritually

In 1 Samuel 16:23, the evil spirit departed from Saul as a result of David's music. That's not a magic formula for getting rid of evil spirits, but we do learn that music can be a source of spiritual restoration to someone who is spiritually depressed. God has given us a wonderful gift in music, and, when properly used, it can bring refreshment to the mind, healing to the body, and restoration to the spirit.

QUESTION 4: How Do Believers Sing?

"Speaking . . . singing and making melody."

A. The General Statement

The Greek word for "speaking" is *laleō*, which refers to the movement of the tongue or any sound from the mouth. It is an onomatopoetic word that originated from the chatter or babble of children, such as "la, la, la." It was also used of the chirp of birds or the grunts and other noises of animals. In classical Greek, *laleō* is used of the noise of the grasshopper or cricket.

1. Revelation 4:1—The apostle John said, "I looked and, behold, a door was opened in heaven; and the first voice that I heard was, as it were, of a trumpet talking with me; which said, Come up here, and I will show thee things which must be hereafter." *Laleō* is used here to refer to a musical instrument.

2. Revelation 10:4—John said, "When the seven thunders had uttered their voices, I was about to write." Here the same word is used of the voice of thunder.

Speaking as defined in Ephesians 5:19 includes any sound offered to God from a Spirit-filled heart. The music from a guitar or a homemade flute is as acceptable to God as the music from an organ or choir.

B. The Specific Statements

1. Singing songs

The Greek word for "singing" is *adō*, which simply means "to sing with the voice." I have met some groups in Christian circles who believe you shouldn't have choirs. But one of the best ways to make music is to sing with your voice. It is an act of worship when someone sings from his heart to the Lord. Choirs are seen throughout the Bible. You may not have a good singing voice, but that isn't the issue—what matters is the heart. Believers are commanded to sing with their voices to the Lord. I believe the human voice is the most beautiful instrument God ever created. Because of its flexibility, God has created an incredible tool for believers to praise Him. If you are controlled by the Spirit of God, you have the right to sing to your heart's content. Whether you sing at a Bible study, in a church service, with your family, or even in the shower, sing to glorify God.

2. Making melody

"Making melody" is an unfortunate translation of verse 19, because the actual meaning in the Greek text is somewhat different. The Greek word is *psallō*, which at its root means "to pluck." The English word *psalm* comes from this Greek word and includes the idea of plucking on a stringed instrument, particularly a harp. *Psallō* came to represent the making of any instrumental music. Some churches in America have taught that musical instruments are sinful and should not be allowed in the church. But this portion of Scripture counters that notion, because God is honored by beautiful music played and sung in His holy name. The Spirit-filled heart can express itself in any sort of vocal or instrumental music. The apostle Paul is saying there are two ways to praise God in song—with the voice and with instruments.

QUESTION 5: In What Ways Should We Sing?

"In psalms and hymns and spiritual songs."

A. Psalms

"Psalms" (Gk., *psalmōs*) refers primarily to the Old Testament psalms put to music. It is sometimes used in a broad sense to refer to anthems to God. Luke, however, used it exclusively to refer to the Psalms (cf. Acts 13:33; Luke 24:44). The early church did most of its singing directly from the psalter, using various tunes familiar to the congregation—a pattern followed for hundreds of years by many European and American churches and still used in some congregations today. The psalms primarily speak of the nature and work of God, especially in the lives of believers. They are designed to magnify and glorify God.

B. Hymns

The Greek word *humnos* for "hymns," literally means "a song of praise." That concept of hymn is frequently connected with the work of Jesus Christ. Many biblical scholars believe that various New Testament passages such as Colossians 1:12-16 and Philippians 2:6-11 were used as hymns in the early church. They were directed at the redemptive work of Christ. Whereas the psalms were devoted to the character and work of God, the hymns in the New Testament have centered on the work of Christ on the cross.

C. Spiritual Songs

"Spiritual songs" were like testimonies in the early church. The adjective "spiritual" implies that such songs conveyed the singer's changed life in expressing spiritual truth. So in the church today, classic renditions of psalms 23 and 84 would be considered psalms, "A Mighty Fortress Is Our God" and "The Old Rugged Cross" would be considered hymns, and "O How He Loves You and Me" and "I'd Rather Have Jesus" would be considered spiritual songs. Paul is not trying to classify or regulate all music in the church; he is simply giving latitude for all kinds of musical expression to exalt the Lord. Whether songs are great hymns about God and the cross of Christ or recitations of testimony, all are the expressions of a Spirit-filled heart.

The church today faces a crisis in Christian music. Many people are using music in Jesus' name just to make money. They are singing, but their hearts aren't right with God. Some of their songs convey unbiblical thoughts and unsound theology or attempt to drag Jesus down to the level of a buddy or pal. Because of their improper motives, they are not unlike Simon Magus, who tried to buy the Holy Spirit's power for his own magic act (Acts 8:9-24).

Conclusion

Jesus said to His Father, "I will declare thy name unto my brethren [believers], in the midst of the church will I sing praise unto thee" (Heb. 2:12). Do you know who the greatest soloist in the universe is? Jesus! God has chosen to use believers as channels for Christ to do His work. As Christians are filled with the Holy Spirit and as the joy of the Lord wells up within them, then and only then can they offer their songs of praise to God. Although doing so is a joy inexpressible, it is also a solemn responsibility. When you quench the Spirit, you also quench the song of Christ to the Father.

Focusing on the Facts

1. What is the key for all of Jesus' promises to believers (see p. 88)?
2. What is the promise for the believer's inheritance? How is it fulfilled? (see p. 89)?
3. What is the promise concerning the believer's works? How is it fulfilled (see pp. 89-90)?

4. What promise of Jesus affects the believer's prayer life (see p. 90)?
5. In what way is Galatians 5:22 a fulfillment of Jesus' promises in John 13-15 (see pp. 91-92)?
6. All music is to be offered to _____ (see p. 93).
7. Of what must believers remind themselves when singing (see p. 94)?
8. What are three profitable effects of music? Explain your answer (see pp. 94-96).
9. What is the general statement regarding how believers should sing (see pp. 96-97)?
10. The apostle Paul said there are two ways to make sounds that praise and glorify God. What are they (Ephesians 5:19; see p. 97)?
11. Explain the difference between psalms, hymns, and spiritual songs (see pp. 98-99).
12. What specific problem is the church facing today concerning Christian music (see p. 99)?
13. What is Jesus communicating to God the Father when Spirit-filled believers sing to God (see p. 99)?

Pondering the Principles

1. Jesus promised believers many things, including a future inheritance, fruitful works, answered prayer, and the indwelling Holy Spirit. They are all brought to fruition by the coming of the Holy Spirit into the believer's life. Do you sense the presence of the Holy Spirit in your life? Do you live this Spirit-controlled life on a daily basis? Are you aware of Christ's promises being confirmed by the Spirit in your daily activities? Memorize 2 Peter 1:3-4, and then begin to search the Scriptures for "His precious and magnificent promises."

2. Scripture is replete with verses that describe a joyful saint as a singing saint. Are you so controlled by the Holy Spirit that your heart longs to sing to the Lord? Is singing ever a part of your life, whether public or private? Take time now to ask the Holy Spirit to guide your life. As a result of His leading, begin to cultivate an attitude of thankfulness for all that God has done in your life, and then praise Him with song.

7
Be Filled with the Spirit—Part 4

Outline

Introduction
A. The Key for Christian Living
B. The Key for Christian Leaders
C. The Key for Church Renewal

Review
 I. The Contrast (v. 18*a*)
 II. The Command (v. 18*b*)
III. The Consequences (vv. 19-21)
    A. The Inward Result—Singing (v. 19)

Lesson
B. The Upward Result—Saying Thanks to God (v. 20)
    1. The source of thanksgiving
        a) Job 1:21
        b) 2 Corinthians 4:15
        c) 2 Corinthians 9:11-12, 15
    2. The specifics of thanksgiving
        a) When are believers to be thankful?
            (1) Thankfulness after a trial
                (*a*) Exodus 14:31
                (*b*) Revelation 15:1-3
            (2) Thankfulness before a trial
            (3) Thankfulness during a trial
        b) For what are we to be thankful?
            (1) The reason
            (2) The reality
        c) How are we to be thankful?
            (1) The contrast
            (2) The culmination

d) To whom do we give thanks?
  (1) The precepts
  (2) The pattern
3. The scope of thanksgiving
  a) The parable of the rich fool
  b) The parable of the Pharisee and the tax collector
  c) The account of the ten lepers
C. The Outward Result—Submitting (v. 21)

Introduction

A. The Key for Christian Living

The key to living the Christian life is being controlled on a daily basis by the Holy Spirit. When believers are not filled or controlled by the Spirit of God, there is no progress. Since each true believer is indwelt by the Holy Spirit (Rom. 8:9), it is imperative that each true believer yield his life moment-by-moment to the Spirit. The apostle Paul scolded the Galatians by saying, "Are ye so foolish? Having begun in the Spirit, are ye now made perfect [mature] in the flesh?" (Gal. 3:3). Since believers are born again of the Spirit (John 3:5-7), renewed by the Spirit (Titus 3:5), and are the temple of the Spirit (1 Cor. 6:19), it is foolish to disregard the Spirit's work and try to live in the flesh. As Paul implies, having begun in the Spirit, we will become mature only in the Spirit.

B. The Key for Christian Leaders

The key leaders in the New Testament were all filled with the Holy Spirit.

1. Jesus Christ

Luke 4:1 says, "Jesus, being full of the Holy Spirit, returned from the Jordan, and was led by the Spirit into the wilderness." Likewise, John 3:34 says, "God giveth not the Spirit by measure unto him." Jesus accomplished His earthly ministry by the power of the Spirit of God (e.g., Matt. 12:28).

2. John the Baptist

   John the Baptist, the forerunner of our Lord, was the greatest man who ever lived up until his time (Matt. 11:11). Luke says, "He shall be filled with the Holy Spirit, even from his mother's womb" (Luke 1:15). Both John the Baptist's mother, Elisabeth, and father, Zacharias, were filled with the Holy Spirit (Luke 1:41, 67).

3. Peter

   Acts 4:8 says the great apostle Peter was "filled with the Holy Spirit." He was filled with the Holy Spirit as he preached at Pentecost and here as he addressed the Sanhedrin.

4. Stephen

   Stephen, one of the first officials of the early church, was chosen because he was "full of faith and of the Holy Spirit" (Acts 6:5). Verse 3 says that any who desired to serve must be "of honest report, full of the Holy Spirit and wisdom." Later, while being stoned, Stephen was "full of the Holy Spirit, [then] looked up steadfastly into heaven, and saw the glory of God, and Jesus standing on the right hand of God" (Acts 7:55).

5. Paul

   The apostle Paul met Jesus on the road to Damascus and was blinded. Afterward a believer came up to him and said, "Brother Saul, the Lord, even Jesus, that appeared unto thee in the way as thou camest, hath sent me, that thou mightest receive thy sight, and be filled with the Holy Spirit" (Acts 9:17). Acts 13:9 says, "Saul (who is also called Paul), [was] filled with the Holy Spirit."

6. Barnabas

   Barnabas traveled with the apostle Paul and was known for his gift of exhortation. Acts 11:24 says, "He was a righteous man, and full of the Holy Spirit."

Ever since the earliest days of the church and even before, the concept of the filling of the Spirit has been central. When believers yield the control of their lives to the Spirit of God, what was said of the disciples will be said of them: "These . . . have turned the world upside down" (Acts 17:6). Being controlled by the Holy Spirit releases God's divine power, enabling believers to do great things for God. Jesus said regarding those filled with the Spirit, "He that believeth on me, the works that I do shall he do also; and greater works than these shall he do, because I go unto my Father" (John 14:12). Likewise Paul said, "Unto him who is able to do exceedingly abundantly above all that we ask or think, according to the power that worketh within us" (Eph. 3:20). When self-will is jettisoned, sin is confessed, and obedience is maintained, only then is the believer controlled by the Spirit of God.

C. The Key for Church Renewal

There has been a great effort recently to recapture the meaning and effectiveness of the early church. The key to reproducing the power of the early church is not necessarily duplicating its methodology but being controlled by the same Holy Spirit who was in the early church. When the church in the twentieth century is controlled by the Spirit of God as was the early church, then the church will be under God's divine direction.

Review

I. THE CONTRAST (v. 18a; see pp. 7-17)

II. THE COMMAND (v. 18b; see pp. 55-67, 73-76)

III. THE CONSEQUENCES (vv. 19-21)

A. The Inward Result—Singing (v. 19; see pp. 76-84, 92-99)

Lesson

B. The Upward Result—Saying Thanks to God (v. 20)

"Giving thanks always for all things unto God and the Father in the name of our Lord Jesus Christ."

A Spirit-filled believer gives thanks to God for everything. Psalm 100:4 declares, "Enter into his [God's] gates with thanksgiving, and into his courts with praise; be thankful unto him, and bless his name." Commentator William Hendriksen said that when a person prays without thanksgiving, he has clipped the wings of prayer so that it cannot rise.

1. The source of thanksgiving

I believe being thankful is the single greatest act of personal worship a Christian can render to God. Thankfulness is the epitome of true spiritual worship. Worship does not necessarily require stained glass windows, organ music, or singing great hymns in church, though those things may enhance it. The highest and ultimate act in worship is to possess a thankful heart, recognizing God as the source of everything. The ability to offer thanks in the midst of any situation, good or bad, is the ability to praise God. A thankful heart sees beyond the difficult circumstances to the sovereignty of God (cf. Rom. 8:28). Thankfulness helps conform the believer to the image of Jesus Christ because it causes him to see God working out everything for good regardless of the difficult circumstances.

a) Job 1:21—Job said, "Naked came I out of my mother's womb, and naked shall I return there. The Lord gave, and the Lord hath taken away; blessed be the name of the Lord." Job thanked God when He gave but also when He took away. Job had a mature perspective in seeing God as the source of everything.

105

b) 2 Corinthians 4:15—Paul said, "All things are for your sakes, that the abundant grace might through the thanksgiving of many redound to the glory of God." Everything God does is for the believer's good, whether a blessing or trial. We glorify God when we recognize that fact. Only then is a believer able to say, "God, no matter how much this situation hurts, I want to be thankful to You in spite of it."

c) 2 Corinthians 9:11-12, 15—Paul said, "Being enriched in everything to all bountifulness, which causeth through us thanksgiving to God. For the administration of this service not only supplieth the want of the saints, but is abundant also by many thanksgivings unto God. . . . Thanks be unto God for his unspeakable gift." The ultimate response to what God has done in the life of a believer is thanksgiving. God has done all that He has that we might be thankful to Him. When we thank God, we give Him glory.

2. The specifics of thanksgiving

Ephesians 5:20 answers several specific questions about the character of true thanksgiving.

a) When are believers to be thankful?

"Always."

Some might say, "But you don't know my problem." This verse, however, does not qualify itself with any special circumstances. The Christian is to be forever thankful to God regardless of his situation. Why? Because a thankful attitude recognizes that God is in complete control. His objective is to conform the believer to the image of Jesus Christ through *everything* that occurs in his life. As a result God receives the glory that is rightfully His. The apostle Paul said, "In everything give thanks; for this is the will of God in Christ Jesus concerning you" (1 Thess. 5:18). If you do not understand what God is trying to accomplish by a certain trial or circumstance in your life, trust that, as you obey Him in everything, it is His will that you persevere with thanksgiving. In Ephesians 5:17

Paul says, "Be ye not unwise but understanding what the will of the Lord is," and His will is clearly revealed in verse 20: "Giving thanks always." God's will for every believer is that he be forever thankful.

Shakespeare's King Lear said, "Ingratitude, thou marble-hearted fiend. . . . How sharper than a serpent's tooth it is to have a thankless child!" (IV. 263, 312). If Shakespeare recognized the detestable nature of ingratitude, imagine how God must feel. Should a believer complain when God brings difficulties and trials into his life, it destroys what God is attempting to accomplish. It renders James 1:2-4 meaningless: "My brethren, count it all joy when ye fall into various trials, knowing this, that the testing of your faith worketh patience. But let patience have her perfect work, that ye may be perfect and entire, lacking nothing." The will of God is that you be thankful so that He can accomplish His perfect work in your life.

(1) Thankfulness after a trial

Many people are thankful only after God has blessed them. It is easy to be thankful after experiencing a blessing. Although it is easy, God does expect that kind of thankfulness.

(a) Exodus 14:31—After the Lord delivered the children of Israel, Scripture says, "Israel saw that great work which the Lord did upon the Egyptians: and the people feared the Lord, and believed the Lord and his servant Moses." They were so thankful, they sang unto the Lord: "Then sang Moses and the children of Israel this song unto the Lord, and spoke, saying, I will sing unto the Lord, for he hath triumphed gloriously: the horse and his rider hath he thrown into the sea. The Lord is my strength and song, and he is become my salvation; he is my God, and I will prepare him an habitation; my father's God, and I will exalt him" (Ex. 15:1-2). The singing was an expression of thanksgiving after the blessing.

(b) Revelation 15:1-3—In recounting his vision, the apostle John's said, "I saw another sign in heaven, great and marvelous, seven angels having the seven last plagues; for in them is filled up the wrath of God. And I saw, as it were, a sea of glass mingled with fire, and them that had gotten the victory over the beast, and over his image, and over his mark, and over the number of his name, standing on the sea of glass, having the harps of God. And they sing the song of Moses, the servant of God, and the song of the Lamb, saying, Great and marvelous are thy works, Lord God Almighty; just and true are thy ways, thou King of saints." That describes the martyred saints in the Tribulation who will gain victory over the Antichrist. They will sing that the victory is over and the battle is won. It will be a time of great thanksgiving. There will always be times of great thanksgiving after a battle is won, but there should also be times of great thanksgiving even beforehand.

(2) Thankfulness before a trial

This is the ability to give thanks to God before the battle begins. It is thankfulness in anticipation of victory. This is where true faith enters the scene. It is believing God before anything happens.

In John 11:39-44 Jesus thanks God at the beginning of a difficult situation. While everyone around Him was crying, He said, "Take away the stone. Martha, the sister of him that was dead, saith unto him, Lord, by this time he stinketh; for he hath been dead four days. Jesus saith unto her, Said I not unto thee that, if thou wouldest believe, thou shouldest see the glory of God? Then they took away the stone from the place where the dead was laid. And Jesus lifted up his eyes, and said, Father, I thank thee that thou hast heard me. And I knew that thou hearest me always; but, because of the people who stand by I said it, that they may believe that thou hast sent me. And when he thus had spoken, he cried with a loud voice, Lazarus, come forth. And he that was dead came forth, bound hand and foot with graveclothes; and his face was bound about with a cloth. Jesus saith unto them, Loose him, and let him go."

This is a classic example of thanking God in advance. When you see a trial coming, you can believe God for the victory before it ever arrives. When someone falls apart in anticipation of a potential problem, he hasn't reached the level of maturity God desires. It is easy to thank God after the blessing but much harder to thank Him before the trial begins.

(3) Thankfulness during a trial

It is hardest of all to thank God in the midst of a difficult trial. Doing so is indicative of true Christian character. Throughout the Bible, God's choice people have always been able to give thanks—even in the most impossible situations.

(a) Daniel 6:10—King Darius sent out a decree stating that no one could be worshiped or prayed to except him, but "when Daniel knew that the writing was signed, he went into his house; and his windows being open in his chamber toward Jerusalem, he kneeled upon his knees three times a day, and prayed, and gave thanks before his God, as he did previously." Daniel was thrown into a lions' den as a result, but God honored his thankful spirit by sparing his life.

(b) Jonah 2:1-10—Jonah "prayed unto the Lord, his God, out of the fish's belly, and said, I cried by reason of mine affliction unto the Lord, and he heard me; out of the belly of sheol cried I, and thou heardest my voice. For thou hadst cast me into the deep, in the midst of the seas, and the floods compassed me about; all thy billows and thy waves passed over me. Then I said, I am cast out of thy sight; yet I will look again toward thine holy temple. The waters compassed me about, even to the soul; the depth closed me round about, the weeds were wrapped about my head. I went down to the bottoms of the mountains; the earth, with its bars, was about me forever; yet hast thou brought up my life from corruption, O Lord, my God. When my soul fainted within me, I remembered the Lord; and my prayer came in unto thee, into thine holy temple. They that observe lying vanities forsake their own mercy. But I will sacrifice unto thee with the voice of thanksgiving; I will pay that that I have vowed. Salvation is of the Lord. And the Lord spoke unto the fish, and it vomited out Jonah upon the dry land."

Could you ever possibly imagine yourself in Jonah's situation—floating about in the acidic stomach of a huge fish? And even worse, to be alive and awake in the belly of that fish! But in the midst of his difficulty, Jonah thanked the Lord for his problem, and God responded to his prayer. He honored Jonah's thankfulness.

(c) Hebrews 12:3-4—Hebrews 11 is a chapter dedicated to those who thanked God in the midst of terrible trials. The writer of Hebrews then turned to those to whom he was writing and said, "Ye have not resisted unto blood, striving against sin" (Heb. 12:4). He was encouraging those who had not suffered such terrible tragedies to thank God in the midst of their own trials.

(d) Acts 5:40-42—Luke said, "When they [the Sanhedrin] had called the apostles, and beaten them, they commanded that they should not speak in the name of Jesus, and let them go. And they departed from the presence of the council, rejoicing that they were counted worthy to suffer shame for his name. And daily in the Temple, and in every house, they ceased not to teach and preach Jesus Christ." The apostles were thankful to God in the midst of their beatings.

(e) Acts 16:25—Luke said, "At midnight Paul and Silas prayed, and sang praises unto God; and the prisoners heard them." With their hands and feet stretched as far as they could be and locked in stocks, they thanked God in the midst of their situation.

(f) Philippians 1:12-14, 18—Paul said, "I would ye should understand, brethren, that the things which happened unto me have fallen out rather unto the furtherance of the gospel, so that my bonds in Christ are manifest in all the palace, and in all other places; and many of the brethren in the Lord, becoming confident by my bonds, are much more bold to speak the word without fear. . . . Notwithstanding, every way, whether in pretense or in truth, Christ is preached; and in that I do rejoice, yea, and will rejoice." Even though Paul was a prisoner and being persecuted, his heart was filled with thanksgiving.

How a believer gives thanks is indicative of his spiritual maturity. If a Christian gives thanks to God only after a blessing or trial, he has reached only the first level of thanksgiving. If he can thank God before the trial, he shows a higher level of maturity. If, however, he can thank God in the midst of the trial, he has reached the level of maturity few Christians ever know. One such Christian, Joni Eareckson Tada, wrote about her experience after an accident that paralyzed her (recounted in *Joni* [Grand Rapids: Zondervan, 1976]). She learned that giving thanks is not a matter of feeling thankful; it's a matter of obedience. You don't always have to feel thankful; true spiritual maturity is a matter of recognizing that your entire life and circumstances are in God's sovereign hand. Everything that happens is simply God's working out His purpose—conforming the believer to the image of Jesus Christ.

b) For what are we to be thankful?

"All things."

(1) The reason

The believer is to be thankful for everything, including the goodness and mercy of God (Pss. 106:1; 107:1; 136:1-3), the gift of Christ (2 Cor. 9:15), Christ's power and reign (Rev. 11:17), the reception and effectual working of the Word of God in others (1 Thess. 2:13; 3:9), deliverance through Christ from indwelling sin (Rom. 7:23-25), victory over death and the grave (1 Cor. 15:57), wisdom and might (Dan. 2:23), the triumph of the gospel (2 Cor. 2:14), the conversion of others (Rom. 6:17), faith exhibited by others (Rom. 1:8; 2 Thess. 1:3), love exhibited by others (2 Thess. 1:3), grace bestowed on others (1 Cor. 1:4; Phil. 1:3-5; Col. 1:3-6), the zeal exhibited by others (2 Cor. 8:16), the nearness of God's presence (Ps. 75:1), appointment to the ministry (1 Tim. 1:12), willingness to offer our resources for God's service (1 Chron. 29:6-14), and the supply of our bodily wants (Rom. 14:6-7; 1 Tim. 4:3-4). In short, we're to be thankful for all men (1 Tim. 2:1) and all things (2 Cor. 9:11; Eph. 5:20), including trouble (James 1:2-4).

(2) The reality

Only a humble person can be thankful for everything. He knows he deserves nothing and therefore gives thanks even for the smallest things. Lack of thankfulness comes from pride and thinking you deserve better. Pride tries to convince people that their jobs, health, and spouses are not as good as they deserve. Pride was the root of the first sin and remains the root of all sin. Satan's pride led him to rebel against God. The pride of

112

Adam and Eve led them to believe Satan's lie that they deserved more than they had, even the right to be as God.

Believers are still subject to the temptations of pride. The only cure is humility, and that comes from being filled with the Spirit. Humility dethrones self and enthrones Christ, and in so doing thankfully acknowledges that every good thing—including many things that do not at the time seem to be good—is from His gracious hand.

c) How are we to be thankful?

"In the name of our Lord Jesus Christ."

The believer's thankfulness is to be consistent with who Christ is and what He has done. Regardless of what occurs in a believer's life, he can still be thankful, because Christ is working out His perfect will and deserves all the glory. Christ says thanks to the Father through the believer because He gives the believer the capacity to be thankful.

(1) The contrast

A person who is not a Christian doesn't have Christ interceding on his behalf at the right hand of God or the Holy Spirit indwelling his life. Likewise he does not have the promise of joint-heirship with Christ or citizenship in God's kingdom. Since a nonbeliever has no indwelling Holy Spirit, he therefore is not filled by Him. He is not granted any of the wonderful promises made by Christ. He therefore cannot be thankful and has no assurance that everything is working out for his good, as the believer has (Rom. 8:28). He ends up seeking only present, not eternal, glory.

The child of God, however, *is* indwelt by Christ, *is* a joint-heir with Him, and *does* have the Son interceding for him at the Father's right hand. He has all of Christ's promises made certain through the Holy Spirit who indwells him. And as the

Spirit controls him, he is cleansed from sin and made progressively more like Christ Himself. Since all this is true, the believer has every cause to be wholly thankful to God.

(2) The culmination

By nature, man is utterly self-seeking, and when he doesn't feel he got what he deserved, he becomes ingratitude personified. But the mature Christian, who is filled with the Spirit, becomes thankful as Christ Himself was thankful. In His earthly ministry, Jesus was continually giving thanks to His Father (cf. Matt. 11:25; 26:27; John 6:11, 23; 11:41). Before He multiplied the loaves and fish to feed the four thousand, "He gave thanks and broke them, and started giving them to His disciples to serve to them" (Mark 8:6, NASB). Even as He instituted the Lord's Supper in the shadow of the cross, He thanked His Father for the bread that would soon become a memorial of His sacrificed body (Luke 22:19).

Jesus left His glory in heaven and came to earth to humble Himself and become a servant. He was spat upon, ridiculed, despised, scorned, rejected, blasphemed, beaten, and finally crucified. Yet because of His great humility He always gave thanks in all things. He didn't deserve any of the ill-treatment He received, yet He was thankful. He deserved glory but received humiliation, He deserved love but received hate, He deserved worship but received rejection, He deserved praise but received scorn, He deserved riches but became poor, and He deserved holiness but He was made sin on our behalf. Jesus never ceased giving thanks to God because He could see the ultimate end in view—the cross. Hebrews 12:2 says we're to be "looking unto Jesus, the author and finisher of our faith, who for the joy that was set before him endured the cross, despising the shame, and is set down at the right hand of the throne of God."

Because Jesus emptied Himself to the point of giving His own life (cf. Phil. 2:7-8), He is able to fill believers with everything He emptied Himself of, including life. We deserve humiliation, and yet in Christ we receive glory. We deserve to be hated, but in Christ we receive divine love; we deserve to be rejected, but in Christ we receive sonship; we deserve scorn, but in Christ we receive affection; we deserve poverty, yet He gives us His riches; and we deserve sin's curse, yet He imparts to us His own righteousness—and we receive eternal life! For what can we not give thanks?

d) To whom do we give thanks?

"Unto God and the Father."

Believers should thank their heavenly Father just as the Lord Himself did on earth. The apostle Paul used the term *Father* because he was emphasizing the benevolent aspect of God, who continually bestows gifts to His own. James said, "Every good gift and every perfect gift is from above, and cometh down from the Father of lights, with whom is no variableness, neither shadow of turning" (1:17). The Giver of these perfect gifts should also then be the Receiver of genuine and heartfelt thanks. We are to thank our beneficent Father for all things, because He has given us all things (cf. Eph. 1:3).

Once when I gave a gift to someone who was in need, I received from him a note entirely thanking God. I was thrilled to see that that person recognized the real giver—God Himself—and not simply the channel for that gift. He correctly recognized God as the actual source of all things. Thanking a human being is by no means wrong, but when a believer sees God as the source of everything, then he has the perspective of Ephesians 5:20.

(1) The precepts

A distinguishing characteristic of unsaved people is thanklessness. Paul states in Romans 1:21, "When they knew God, they glorified him not as God, neither were thankful." The true mark of a Spirit-controlled believer is a heart thankful toward God. The Old Testament is replete with examples of those who were thankful to God (Pss. 30:4, 12; 50:14; 69:30; 92:1; 95:2; 100:4; 116:17). Certain orders of Levitical priests had no other duty but to lead the people in thanksgiving (cf. 1 Chron. 16:4, 7-36; 23:27-30; 2 Chron. 31:2). The various feasts of Israel were designed to cultivate a spirit of thankfulness and praise. The Feasts of Pentecost, Trumpets, Tabernacles, Lights, and Purim were great national acts of thanksgiving to God, who had served His people so lovingly and graciously.

(2) The pattern

Likewise, in the New Testament God calls all believers to be thankful. Paul said to the Philippians, "Be anxious for nothing, but in everything, by prayer and supplication with thanksgiving, let your requests be made known unto God" (4:6). And he said to the Colossians, "As ye have, therefore, received Christ Jesus the Lord, so walk ye in him, rooted and built up in him, and established in the faith, as ye have been taught, abounding with thanksgiving" (2:6-7). The writer of Hebrews commands, "Let us offer the sacrifice of praise to God continually, that is, the fruit of our lips giving thanks to his name" (Heb. 13:15).

3. The scope of thanksgiving

a) The parable of the rich fool

Some people are not thankful simply because they think they deserve every good thing they have—and more. They think that thanksgiving is unnecessary. Jesus said, "The ground of a certain rich man brought forth plentifully. And he thought within himself, saying, What shall I do, because I have no place to bestow my crops? And he said, This will I do: I will pull down my barns, and build greater; and there will I bestow all my crops and my goods. And I will say to my soul, Soul, thou hast much goods laid up for many years; take thine ease. Eat, drink, and be merry. But God said unto him, Thou fool, this night thy soul shall be required of thee; then whose shall those things be, which thou hast provided? So is he that layeth up treasure for himself, and is not rich toward God" (Luke 12:16-21).

The rich farmer of Jesus' parable was presumptuous about his future prosperity and ungrateful for his past prosperity. He didn't think he owed God anything because he didn't acknowledge that God was the source of all his wealth. He assumed he had amassed all the wealth himself. Within Christ's judgment lay the truth that the farmer could no more protect his possessions by his own power than he had produced them by his own power. What the rich farmer didn't realize was that unless God made the grain grow, he would have had nothing. Not feeling the need to thank God is much worse than ingratitude—it essentially is unbelief. Failing to acknowledge God is practical atheism.

b) The parable of the Pharisee and the tax collector

Other people thank themselves while under the guise that they are thanking God, but that is hypocrisy. Jesus "spoke this parable unto certain who trusted in themselves that they were righteous, and despised others: Two men went up into the temple to pray; the one a Pharisee, and the other a tax collector. The Pharisee stood and prayed thus with himself, God, I thank thee that I am not as other men are, extortioners, unjust, adulterers, or even as this tax collector. I fast twice in the week; I give tithes of all that I possess. And the tax collector, standing afar off, would not lift up so much as his eyes unto heaven, but smote upon his breast, saying, God be merciful to me a sinner. I tell you, this man went down to his house justified rather than the other; for everyone that exalteth himself shall be abased; and he that humbleth himself shall be exalted" (Luke 18:9-14).

Although the Pharisee used God's name, his thankfulness was to himself and for himself. He was calling attention to his false piety. And because God had no part in his prayer, it was totally worthless. The humble, penitent tax-collector went home justified whereas the proud, self-righteous Pharisee did not. Like the rest of his life, the Pharisee's prayer of thanksgiving was hypocritical pretense.

c) The account of the ten lepers

Luke said of Jesus, "It came to pass, as he went to Jerusalem, that he passed through the midst of Samaria and Galilee. And as he entered into a certain village, there met him ten men that were lepers, who stood afar off. And they lifted up their voices, and said, Jesus, Master, have mercy on us. And when he saw them, he said unto them, Go show yourselves unto the priests. And it came to pass that, as they went, they were cleansed. And one of them, when he saw that he was healed, turned back, and with a loud voice glorified God, and fell down on his face at his feet, giving him thanks; and he was a Samaritan. And Jesus, answering, said, Were there not ten cleansed? But where are the nine? There are not found that returned to give glory to God, except this stranger. And he said unto him, Arise, go thy way; thy faith hath made thee well" (17:11-19).

The Samaritan was considered an outcast in Jesus' day, but he was the only one who received true forgiveness. All ten lepers were healed of their physical disease, but only one received salvation. It is apparent the other nine lepers sought Jesus only for physical healing. The Samaritan in contrast gave glory to God. His thankfulness was an expression of his trust in Christ. He recognized he was utterly helpless in himself and that his healing was undeserved and entirely by God's grace. Gratitude is man at his best; ingratitude is man at his worst. The Spirit-filled believer will not only be thankful but also say as King David said, "I may proclaim with the voice of thanksgiving, and declare all Thy wonders" (Ps. 26:7, NASB).

C. The Outward Result—Submitting (v. 21)

"Submitting yourselves one to another in the fear of God."

Note: The outward result of submitting to one another is expounded in great detail in the study guide entitled *The Fulfilled Family.* It is illustrated in the relationships between husbands and wives (Eph. 5:22-33), children and parents (6:1-4), and slaves and masters (6:5-9).

A Heart of Thanksgiving

A missionary in London was called to an old tenement building where a woman lay during the last stages of a terrible disease. The room was cold and small, and the woman had nowhere to lie but on the floor. When the missionary asked if there was anything he could do, she said, "I have all I really need; I have Christ!" Hearing that account, someone wrote:

> In the heart of London City,
>   'Mid the dwellings of the poor,
> These bright, golden words were uttered,
>   "I have Christ! What want I more?"
> Spoken by a lonely woman,
>   Dying on a garret floor,
> Having not one earthly comfort—
>   "I have Christ! What want I more?"

Focusing on the Facts

1. What is the key to living the Christian life (see p. 102)?
2. Having begun in the Spirit, we will become _____ only in the Spirit (see p. 102).
3. Name the key leaders in the New Testament who were characterized as being filled with the Holy Spirit. Support your answer with Scripture (see pp. 102-3).

4. Being controlled by the Holy Spirit releases God's _____ _____ enabling believers to do great things for God (see p. 104).
5. What must occur for believers to be controlled by the Spirit of God (see p. 104)?
6. What was the key for church renewal in the first century? What is the key for church renewal today (see p. 104)?
7. True or false: Worship and thankfulness are two unrelated issues (see p. 105).
8. Give examples from Scripture on how the sovereignty of God and the thankfulness of man work in harmony (see p. 105).
9. God's will for every believer is to be forever _____ (see p. 107).
10. Discuss the various times we can be thankful in relation to a trial (see pp. 107-9).
11. What is the hardest attitude to have in the Christian life when in the midst of a trial? Give examples of those in Scripture who had this attitude (see pp. 109-10)?
12. True or false: How a believer gives thanks is indicative of his spiritual maturity (see p. 110).
13. What reasons do believers have to be thankful (see p. 112)?
14. _____ was the root of the first sin and remains the root of all sin (see p. 112).
15. What is meant by thanking God "in the name of our Lord Jesus Christ" (see pp. 113-14)?
16. Contrast the role of the Holy Spirit in the life of the believer and the nonbeliever (see p. 113).
17. How did Jesus express an attitude of thankfulness (see pp. 114-15)?
18. What was the apostle Paul emphasizing when he used the phrase "unto God and the Father" (see p. 115)?
19. When a believer sees God as the _____ of _____, then he has the perspective of Ephesians 5:20 (see p. 115).
20. What do the parable of the rich fool, the parable of the Pharisee and the tax collector, and the account of the ten lepers teach us about thanksgiving (see pp. 116-19)?

Pondering the Principles

1. The believer is to be ever and always thankful to God, because that is His will. So often, though, giving thanks to God is diffi-

cult because specific trials or hardships cause much pain and grief. When are you more likely to express thanks to God: before, during, or after a trial? The hardest time to be thankful to God is during a specific trial. As God brings you through your next trial, begin to thank Him in the midst of it, and ask for strength and courage to grow as a result of His testing.

2. People tend to be either thankless, hypocritical in their offering of thanks, or truly thankful. How about you? Of the three parables described on pages 116-19, which most characterizes your life? Take time now to evaluate your attitude about thanksgiving. Ask God to make you a truly thankful person.

3. Ephesians 5:20 gives four principles for offering thanks. We are to give thanks: (1) always, (2) for all things, (3) in the name of Jesus Christ, (4) to God the Father. Do you always give God thanks for all things? Do you thank God because of who Christ is and what He has done for you? As you offer God thanks in the future, begin to use this four-point check system so that you can better glorify Him.

Scripture Index

Topical Index

Alcoholism. *See* Drinking
Aristotle, 29, 83

Bacchus, 15
Bach, Johann Sebastian, 93
Brown, W. G., 30

Carnality, 55-57
Church, renewal of, 104
Coffee. *See* Drinking
Columella, 30
Communion, corruption of, 16
Congreve, William, 94

Delitzsch, Franz, 25
Democritus, 30
Dionysus, 15
Donovan, Professor, 30
Drinking
    alcoholism and, 10-12, 24-25,
        45
    church leaders and, 41-42, 51
    coffee, 38
    commendation of, 26-27
    controversy over, 10, 22-23
    destructiveness of, 43-46
        mentally, 45
        physically, 45-46
    drunkenness and, 12-17, 22-
        26
    guidelines to use regarding,
        27-49
    habit-forming nature of, 43
    higher standards and, 26-27,
        38-42
    necessity of, 32-33
    offensiveness of, 46-48
    one's conscience and, 49
    pagan view of, 14-17
    preference of, 33

testimony to unbelievers and,
    33, 48
today versus Bible times, 28-
    33
Drugs
    addiction to, 10, 12
    heightened consciousness
        and, 14
Drunkenness. *See* Drinking

Gluttony, control of, 43

Habits, evaluation of, 43
Hanson, Howard, 83
Holy Spirit
    baptism of, 57-58
    every Christian's full posses-
        sion of, 57
    filling of, 7-10, 54
        analogy of, 73-76
        confusion about, 54-55
        counterfeit of, 14-17
        importance of, 102
        meaning of, 10, 18-19, 59-
            63, 72-73
        means of experiencing, 63-
            67
        men who experienced, 102-
            4
        misconceptions about, 55-
            59
        results of, 63-64, 72-73
            being submissive to one
                another, 119
            being thankful to God,
                105-19
            singing to God and oth-
                ers, 76-99. *See also*
                Music
    fruit of, 67, 75, 89-91

127